Tales of Ol
CW00348959

Other counties in this series include:

Tales of
Old Somerset

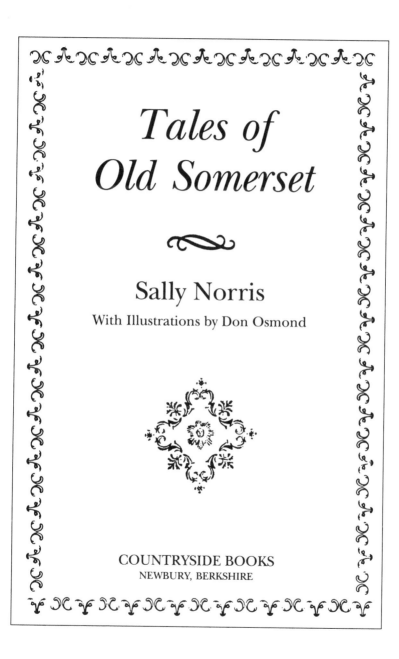

Sally Norris

With Illustrations by Don Osmond

COUNTRYSIDE BOOKS
NEWBURY, BERKSHIRE

First Published 1989
© Sally Norris 1989
Reprinted 1999, 2004

All rights reserved. No reproduction
permitted without the prior permission
of the publishers:

COUNTRY SIDE BOOKS
3 CATHERINE ROAD
NEWBURY, BERKSHIRE

ISBN 1 85306 064 X

Produced through MRM Associates, Reading
Typeset by The LetterWorks Ltd, Reading
Printed in England by J.W. Arrowsmith Ltd., Bristol

For my Parents
Basil and Peggy Speer

Acknowledgements

I am especially grateful to David Bromwich of the Somerset Local History Library at Taunton, the staff of the Westcountry Studies Library at Exeter and Polly Randall of Pilton.

Contents

CONTENTS

SOMERSET: The map overleaf is by John Speede and shows the county as it was in the early seventeenth century.

SOMERSET_SHIRE described.

adinto HUNDREDS devided, with the plott of the famous and most wholsom waters and citie of the BATHE

Part of GLOCESTER SHIRE

BRISTOLL

Part of WILT

SHIRE

Part of Dorset shire

ANNO 1610

West North East South

Cum privilegio

Performed by IOHN SPEEDE and are to be sold
in popes head Alley by Iohn Sudbury et George Humble

The
Cider County

F OR visitors to the county, Somerset has always been
the land of apple trees. Three hundred years ago,
the remarkable Celia Fiennes, who travelled all over Britain on horseback in the 1680s and 1690s wrote:

'In most parts of Sommersetshire it is very fruitfull for
orchards, plenty of apples and peares, but they are not
curious in the planting the best sort of fruite, which is a
great pitty; being so soone produced, and such quan-
tetyes, they are likewise as careless when they make cider,
they press all sorts of apples together....'

Cidermaking is big business in the county - hundreds
of millions of apples are processed each year by the
Taunton Cider Company. But this booming commercial
enterprise developed from a true cottage industry - the
farm cidermakers. For hundreds of years, the farmer
made cider for his own needs and also for his labourers',
from the fruit of his orchard.

He grew standard cider apple trees, planted 40 to the
acre, which reached a height of about 30 ft when mature.
Some famous varieties of the time were *Kingston Black*,
White Sours, *Court of Wick Pippin*, and the cottager's apple

Tom Putt. Sheep and cows grazed under their broad canopies.

In the autumn came the harvest. Usually the fruit was gathered, when it had fallen, by the women and children of the farm, who were quicker workers than the men. The apples were collected into withy (willow) baskets, each holding about 20 pounds. These were emptied into larger baskets called 'maunds' which held about 60 pounds. A good tree, laden with fruit, would fill about ten of these large baskets, so a great deal of bending, stooping, and backache was expected from the pickers.

The apples were usually left to ripen in an apple loft or 'tallet' on a bed of dry straw. When ready, they were cleaned of leaves and twigs and pushed through a hole in the floor of the loft to the wooden apple mill beneath. The hand-operated mill crushed the fruit into small pieces (not too small, as the apples had to retain their juice). The pieces, called 'pomace', were scooped out with a wooden shovel and put into the press, which, like all the cidermaking equipment, was made of wood - any metal parts dissolved and ruined the cider.

Now the expertise of the most experienced cidermaker was needed. He constructed a straw 'cheese' on the bed of the press. Layers of clean, combed wheat straw and pomace were carefully built into a pyramid shape. When the 'cheese' was high enough, a heavy square of wood was placed on top and further blocks of timber added to increase the weight. Then the press was screwed down gradually during the next day or so. About seven gallons of juice could be extracted from a couple of hundredweight of apples. The largest presses held about a ton of pomace, yielding 120 gallons of cider. The juice was ladled out of the trough at the base of the press with a wooden 'dipper', and poured into buckets which in turn were emptied into casks through a funnel or 'tun-nacre'. All sorts of substances might be added at this stage to enhance both colour and flavour, including raspberries, wormwood, beetroot and boiling sugar.

The casks were stored in the ciderhouse, a specially built cellar designed to keep the cider cool. The slower the fermentation, the better the finished product, so for several weeks the bungholes were left open to allow the froth to escape and to enable the cidermaker to top up the cask to exclude any air. Once the froth had died down, the casks were 'bunged down' bit by bit. Great patience was needed at this vital stage; if done in haste, the bung could be blown out and much of the cider wasted. Usually, several months elapsed before the cider was ready to drink.

It was to the ciderhouse that the farmworkers came for their daily ration. But the drink which they received as part of their wages was nothing like the cider that the farmer consumed with his family and friends, made from the first pressing of the apples. The labourers' beverage was made from the second pressing, greatly diluted with water. The result was a weak, sour drink, truthfully described by a 19th century writer as a 'horrible liquor which is given to the labourer under the ironical name of cider'. The reason why the workers were so shabbily treated was an economic one, as Thomas Knight pointed out in *A Treatise on the Culture of the Apple and Pear and on the Manufacture of Cider and Perry* (1809). 'The flavour of the liquor is here a secondary consideration with the farmer; whose first object must be to obtain a large quantity at small expense'. The usual allowance for a labourer was four pints a day, although at harvest time two gallons a day was both needed and expected by those working a 16 hour day.

The most delicious cider, made for the farmer's wife and her friends, had all sorts of extras stirred in, such as sultanas, raisins, oranges, lemons, ginger, cinnamon and brown sugar. The resulting nectar was not only a delight to drink, it also had the agreeable effect of stimulating lots of uninhibited gossip!

Sadly, farmhouse cidermaking, while it has not completely died out, is no longer an integral part of life on the farm. Farmworkers are paid like everyone else, and many of the old orchards have been grubbed out. The big cidermaking firms use apples from new varieties of bush apple trees, planted at the rate of 240 to an acre, six times as many as the old trees. A hundred years ago, 25,000 acres of Somerset were orchard - a truly magnificent sight at blossom time. Nowadays, just a tenth of that is planted with apple trees, but the apple blossom is still a beautiful spectacle even for travellers racing through the county by train.

One world-famous Somerset family still very much involved in the business of producing liquid refreshment is the Showerings. In 1842, Francis Showering was a beer seller in Garston Street, Shepton Mallet, and by 1860, was also brewing beer in Kilver Street. In the 1940s, the family added cidermaking to their other talents. Because of them, Shepton Mallet is known all over the world as the home of Babycham, a drink not of apples, but of perry pears grown in the Showering's own orchards. More than three million bottles are produced each week by a workforce of about 200 - a far cry from the farm cidermakers.

There are a number of fascinating places to visit in the county to see the old apple mills, presses and associated implements, including Sheppy's Cider Museum at Bradford-on-Tone, and Perry's Cider Mills at Dowlish

Wake, near Ilminster. Here, of course, you can sample traditional farmhouse cider at full strength - the 'real thing'. You might also remember the wise words of John Worlidge, writing in his *Vinetum Britannicum* (1676)-

'The constant use of this liquor hath been found by long experience to avail much to health and long life, preserving the Drinkers of it in their full strength and vigour even to very old age.'

Disaster
At Foxcote

O N AUGUST Bank Holiday 1876, a sixteen year old boy named Alfred Dando was arrested. A dozen people had been killed, and it seemed he was responsible.

For those twelve, travelling by rail had not proved to be, as Sydney Smith thought in 1842, 'a delightful improvement of human life', but the end of it. They were victims of the only major accident involving passengers in the colourful 111 year existence of the Somerset & Dorset Railway. But as we shall see, the accident was the lamentable and almost fated outcome of the first twenty-two difficult years in the S & D's chequered history.

The coming of the railways to the remote West Country was outstandingly important to its social and economic development, bringing new employment, new industries such as tourism and horticulture, and easy access to the rest of Great Britain. The sentiments of Sydney Smith, who was rector at Combe Florey from 1829-42, were echoed throughout Somerset. 'Everything is near, everything is immediate - time, distance, and delay are abolished.' The years of Railway Mania were looming on the horizon; in one month in 1845, 357 new schemes were advertised nationally. The Bristol & Exeter

Railway had put Bridgwater on the railway map in 1841, Taunton following a year later.

Somerset's very own railway, the Somerset Central, was launched in 1852 by James Clark of Street, already making wool-lined slippers and eager for his new shoe-making venture to find country-wide markets. The railway opened in August 1854 with a twelve mile stretch of track from the port at Highbridge to Glastonbury, and was ridiculed by critics as 'going from nowhere to nowhere over a turf moor.' By 1859, it was extended to Burnham and Wells - 19 miles of single line track. Although never prosperous, and not even very efficient, the Somerset Central achieved its aim - to provide a service to link the English and Bristol Channels - in 1863, a year after its amalgamation with the Dorset Central. Now known as the Somerset & Dorset Railway, its independent life continued for another 14 years. But it was plagued by lack of money, and lurched from one financial crisis to the next.

In a last-ditch effort to make the line pay, the directors planned an ambitious extension to Bath, connecting with the Midland Railway route to Birmingham. On 20th July 1874, the new line from Bath to Bournemouth was opened. The first train left Bath at 7.25 am, but was greatly delayed by spectators at various points along the way waiting to cheer its progress. The *Bath Chronicle* commented

'May the Somerset & Dorset managers speedily mend their ways in the matter of punctuality or they will only too quickly find that would-be travellers will go by their longer but fairly punctual competitors, rather than by a route where times of arrival are uncertain and delays not improbable....'

17

A few days later, the S & D was landed with its nick-name - the 'Slow and Dirty' Railway. Although its many supporters responded promptly with 'Swift and Delightful', there is no doubt that the first name stuck. Continuing financial worries meant that only essential maintenance was carried out, and rolling stock and track soon showed signs of wear. Lack of trained staff and insufficient revenue were the last two nails in the company's coffin. The great gamble was over - they had to sell out.

Two companies jumped at the chance jointly to take over - the London & South Western and Midland Railways - elbowing the Great Western out of the way with some hasty underhand manoeuvring. On 13th July 1876, a 999 year lease of the S & D was confirmed by Act of Parliament. The LSWR and Midland, fighting against the prejudice that condemned the line as a 'crazy undertaking', were determined to transform it into a thriving and competent one. Although acutely aware of the problems facing them, they could not have foreseen that all the inadequacies would combine, within one month of their taking over responsibility, to cause the catastrophic crash at Foxcote.

It was August Bank Holiday - 7th August 1876. As expected, the line had been extremely congested all day with 16 scheduled excursion trains going to Bath and Bournemouth as well as the regular services. Mr Difford, the Superintendent, arranged a relief train to leave Wimborne for Bath at 7.10 pm, in the wake of a train from Bournemouth. The crossing agent at Glastonbury, Caleb Percy, warned all the stations en route of the 'extra', and should have arranged crossing points ('loops' of double line track where trains could pass each other) on the single line sections.

The 'up' relief train from Wimborne arrived at Radstock, ten miles from its destination, just after 11 o'clock. The stationmaster, Mr Jarrett, attempted to ascertain from Caleb Percy the whereabouts of an excursion train which should have left Bath at 9.15 pm. The two men apparently had some sort of disagreement, resulting in Jarrett ordering the relief train from Wimborne, with Driver Bishop at the controls, to proceed to Foxcote.

The four mile single line section from Radstock to Wellow was controlled by crossing points and signalboxes at each end. The Foxcote signalbox, between the two, had been in operation for a year, serving the colliery siding at Braysdown. Dividing the section was against Board of Trade regulations, which stipulated that there should never be more than one engine in steam at a time between Radstock and Wellow. In the Foxcote signalbox was 16 year old Alfred Dando, a boy who 'could not write or read excellent', and who was hardly strong enough to pull the distant-signal lever properly. As there was no oil, the signal lamps were unlit. The only knowledge that Alfred had of train movements was via his block tele-graph instruments.

Having arrived at Foxcote, Bishop's relief train waited for a few minutes until the earlier train from Bourne-mouth had left Wellow. Dando then showed Bishop a green light and he began to get his engine on the move. He had reached a speed of about 8 mph when he saw, to his horror, another train almost on top of him. This was the 'missing' train from Bath, driven by John Hamlin, which had departed an hour and a half late. Hamlin left Wellow at quarter past eleven, quite unaware of another train on the line. The stationmaster at Wellow, James Sleep, and his telegraph clerk, Arthur Hillard, forgot to warn Dando that the 'down' train was on the way. John Hamlin was on the downhill curve into Foxcote when he

19

saw the lights of the Wimborne train just 25 yards away. He had reduced speed, and was frantically trying to get his engine into reverse when the inevitable head-on collision occurred.

As the trains ploughed into each other, the terrible sounds of destruction were exacerbated by the continuous shrill whistling of the engines. Bishop's engine stayed on the track but Hamlin's was derailed. Thus it was the carriages of Hamlin's train that suffered the worst damage. The first six were utterly demolished, and in these were all the casualties. Twelve people died that night, including the guard and a mother with her tiny baby. A further 28 were injured. Bishop and Hamlin survived the crash. All those who died were local people on their way home after a day out at Bath Regatta. Their bodies were taken to nearby Paglinch Farm for identification.

The responsibility for investigating accidents rested with the Railway Inspectorate, men recruited from the Royal Engineers. Captain Tyler's report observed that 'safety must more or less depend upon strict adherence to simple rules, and on the employment of responsible agents.' He pointed out that dangerous risks are taken

'when signal-lamps cannot be lighted for want of oil; when special trains are run without printed notices, or even proper telegraphic advices; when wrangling takes place, and important messages are improperly checked . . . . and when the duties supposed to be performed by responsible stationmasters are allowed . . . . to devolve upon telegraph-clerks of immature age or experience, employed for long hours . . . . Railway traffic worked under such conditions cannot, whatever the system employed, be expected to be carried on without serious accidents.'

20

He laid the blame on a number of people. The Superintendent was severely criticized; Percy and Jarrett were censured; James Sleep and Arthur Hillard from Wellow were held ultimately guilty. Hillard, just 15 years old, had been on duty over 15 hours, Sleep over 13 hours. Sleep was charged with manslaughter at Taunton Assizes and sent to prison for a year.

The Joint Committee, which had only just taken over the line, was expressly absolved. Alfred Dando, the poor lad in charge of the Foxcote signalbox, who was arrested after the accident, was found to be blameless. Of all those directly involved in the tragic chain of events that night, he was the only one whose actions were completely justified. He was still working on the S & D in 1916, remembered as a 'quiet-spoken man who read his Bible every day'.

The Somerset & Dorset Railway Trust has a museum at Washford, near Watchet, next to the West Somerset Railway line. It boasts fascinating memorabilia of this picturesque cross-country railway, the closure of which in March 1966 marked the end of an era.

The Man Who Went To The Devil

I N THE Middle Ages, stories of a man who sold his soul to the Devil in exchange for supernatural powers took hold all over Europe. Known as Faust or Faustus, he became a legendary figure whose pact with Satan enabled him to perform fantastic wizardry but which also required him to pay the ultimate penalty - eternal damnation. In England, the first important treatment of the legend was Christopher Marlowe's *Tragical History of Doctor Faustus* (1588), which was extremely popular until the middle of the 17th century. Just at this time, there lived in Chard a man whose desire to emulate Faust caused him to be the victim of a practical joke with deadly consequences.

Abraham Mason was the town's bookseller, confectioner and 'Practitioner of Physick and Chirurgery'. He was also a Quaker, albeit a very unsatisfactory one, who, having briefly attended at the Meeting House at the top of High Street on Sundays, attended much more enthusiastically at the public houses on his way home. Staggering through his front door, he was usually greeted with torrents of abuse from his shrewish wife. How he yearned to silence her screeching tongue!

One day in his shop, he was delving into his books on the occult when a customer entered. They struck up a friendly conversation, during which Abraham confided to the man his secret desire to raise the Devil and acquire magic powers. Concluding that his new acquaintance was a learned gentleman, Abraham inquired if he could possibly think of a way to help him achieve his purpose. Although the man tried to dissuade him, even calling in his brother to assist in the argument, the Quaker would not listen. The two brothers left the bookshop with his pleas ringing in their ears. Thus the idea of playing a joke on him came to them.

They decided that they must first gain his confidence in their supposed abilities in the black arts by showing him 'Satan' in disguise. They hid a puppy in a hedge and persuaded the gullible Quaker that if he walked in absolute silence to the hedge he would see the Devil in the shape of a dog. When he glimpsed the puppy he was quite satisfied that they could raise the Devil. They told him that three nights later Satan would materialize to hear his request. Abraham returned home in a state of great excitement.

For the next three days, the brothers worked hard to make ready for the illusion. They enlisted the help of two men to act as 'Devil' and 'friar'. The 'Devil's' costume was a large rug festooned with horsetails, and on his head he was to wear a lantern attached to a furry cap. The 'friar' was appropriately dressed, carrying staff and bell. The place they decided on was the well-known chert and sandstone caves and quarry at Snowdon, about a mile west of town. They located a pit deep enough to conceal the fake Devil and his henchman, and scattered brimstone and gunpowder round its edge. Now they were ready for the fun.

In the evening of the third day, the brothers met Abraham in town and took him to the quarry, arriving at eleven o'clock. With great solemnity, one of the brothers drew strange shapes and circles on the ground, pretending to conjure the Devil. Out of the pit came the dreadful stink and smoke of brimstone. The 'conjuror' began to chant outlandish words in a singsong voice, and from the reeking pit emerged the 'friar' demanding to know who dared invoke Beelzebub. Trying to smother his mirth, the 'conjuror' begged the 'friar' to summon his master from Hell. This the 'friar' did, with many weird incantations. Terrified but fascinated, Abraham gazed awestruck as a large, hairy, grotesquely illuminated figure rose from the underworld, turned to face him and thundered 'What is thy business with me?' The Quaker stammered out his need for power over women's tongues, his craving for possession of the Philosopher's Stone (which medieval alchemists believed could turn base metal into gold), and an urgent wish to be irresistibly attractive to all pretty, buxom girls. In return, he offered himself (after an agreed term of years), together with 40 shillings and a letter written in his own blood.

The tricksters, delighted with the success of their deception, then set light to the gunpowder to frighten him off. But Abraham stood petrified, until the unearthly clanking of chains from deep in the pit, accompanied by ghastly shrieks, propelled him into action. He took to his heels, helped by whippings from a 'ghostly' coachman lurking in the shadows. He leapt straight over a high stile and did not stop his headlong rush until he was back in Chard. A passer-by, seeing him deathly white and shaking, advised him to go straight home to bed. Once there, blankets pulled over his head, he thought he might be safe, but no! From beneath his window came more dreadful howlings and clatterings from the pursuing coachman. His wife, who knew nothing of his nocturnal activities, was convinced that the Devil had come for him. Not until dawn broke did the tumult cease and the poor Quaker fall into exhausted slumber.

For the practical jokers, morning brought the opportunity to spend Abraham's 40 shillings on a lavish breakfast, while they regaled all their chums with the hilarious goings-on at the stone quarry. The news spread like wildfire through the town, gaining embellishments with each retelling. When the Quaker realized how he had been fooled, he was so overcome with fury and embarrassment that he dared not show his face in the bookshop for four months.

However, as time went by, he gradually reappeared around the town, attending at the Meeting House as before. He also began drinking again on his way home. One night, dead drunk, he tumbled down a flight of steps but suffered no harm. Reassured that he had, in fact, been protected from injury by the Devil, he gave up all pretence of being a Quaker, and turned his back on God. Very soon after, alone in the house and tanked up on brandy, he fell headlong downstairs and broke his neck. Would it be unkind to hope that he did, at last, achieve his heart's desire and come face to face with Satan?

A chronicle of Abraham's misdeeds was published in 1680, three years after his sudden demise, entitled *A strange and wonderful (yet true) Relation of the cursed and hellish design of Abraham Mason, a pretended Quaker, to give himself to the Devil, with the means how he would have done it and how strangely he was prevented. Also an Account of his behaviour afterwards and of his strange Death.* There is a copy of it in the British Museum.

Mary, Mary, Quite Contrary

F OR Somerset, the year 1746 was highly eventful. An earthquake and widespread, disastrous cattle plague had caused great distress, compounded by the dreadful news from Culloden that all the officers of the Somerset Regiment had been killed on the battlefield. At Shepton Mallet, a Methodist meeting had generated such ill-feeling among the audience that a riot broke out. In the midst of all this drama, a trial took place in Taunton that set tongues wagging across the country.

At the Michaelmas Quarter Sessions held in Taunton Castle, a most unusual case was brought before the Court. The learned justices scratched their wigs in puzzlement, since the situation they were faced with was unheard of. The prisoner in the dock was a very attractive woman of 25, Mary Hamilton. Dressed as she was in shirt and trousers she made a devastating youth. So successful was her impersonation that a girl from Wells had been happily married to her for the past three months! Indeed, during the course of the trial the girl, Molly Price, insisted she had had no idea that her 'husband' was female and was loath to utter one word against her. What the Court did not realize was that this was the third time that Mary Hamilton had contracted such a marriage.

She was born in August 1721. Her first attachment was to her neighbour, Anne Johnson. This woman, a zealous Methodist, converted her not only to her faith but to less conventional ideas of love. Infatuated with her friend, Mary readily agreed to go to Bristol with her, where they lived together, but the romance came to a sudden end with the arrival of a good-looking young man called Rogers. He swept Anne off her feet and up the aisle before she could change her mind.

Mary, astutely concluding that a man usually gets what he wants, decided to become one. She dressed herself accordingly and altered her name to George. Ironically enough, as soon as she changed sex she attracted the attention of an itinerant preacher. He was so enamoured of the beautiful 'youth' and so insistent in his courtship that she was forced to take action before the frolicsome cleric discovered his mistake by hitting him on the nose, causing copious bleeding. Unnerved by such rough treatment, the unhappy man fell on his knees and prayed aloud for salvation.

Apparently undaunted by this start to her new life, Mary found lodgings with a 40 year old widow and began to woo her. She believed she was making good progress until the widow decided she would rather marry an Irish soldier and kicked her out.

Hardly had she recovered from the disappointment than Mrs Rushford, the ageing relict of a wealthy cheesemonger, fell violently in love with her. Assuming Mary was a lad of about 18, she let 'him' know very quickly what she had in mind, dropping hints of the financial advantages which might ensue if things developed satisfactorily.

This was the moment when Mary first considered

marriage to one of her own sex. Having proposed to the widow, she had no chance to reconsider; it was her turn to be swept up the aisle and down again on the arm of a woman old enough to be her grandmother. At the wedding feast all the usual lewd jests were bandied around, to the great delight of the bride. She was not quite so delighted by the spiteful remarks of her grandson, whose hopes of a big inheritance had suddenly vanished; when one of the guests commented on the bridegroom's lack of beard, he tartly replied that it would be very queer for both partners to have one.

After three days of marriage, the new Mrs Hamilton confided to her best friend highly-coloured details of her conjugal exploits. In fact, the passive behaviour of her spouse was making her rather anxious. Late that night, the bride decided to take the initiative. The screams and curses which resounded through the house soon after woke the grandson in his attic bedroom. Arriving in his grandmother's room, he found her standing in her nightgown, with a piece of shirt in one hand and a lump of hair in the other. Mary was nowhere to be seen. She had whipped on her breeches, grabbed the rest of her clothes and bolted.

Her flight ended in Totnes, where she found new lodgings and set herself up as a doctor. Her very first patient was Miss Ivythorn, a pretty girl and an easy conquest. They were secretly married eight miles away in Ashburton. Three days later the pair returned to Totnes to beg forgiveness of Mr Ivythorn for their hasty wedding. Completely fooled by Mary's disguise, the bride's father bestowed his blessing, and the couple moved into the family home.

For a fortnight all went well, the second Mrs Hamilton having no suspicion that anything was amiss. But one evening Mary drank a little too much and slept a little too heavily. When she awoke, she found her bedfellow in tears, lamenting the discovery she had made. Mary endeavoured to calm her, reminding her that she could have all the pleasures of marriage without the inconveniences, but such modern thinking was alien to the girl, who threatened to reveal all to her father. Once more, Mary was forced to beat a rapid retreat. The enraged papa, in hot pursuit, obtained a warrant for her arrest, but the bird had flown.

Arriving in Wells, she fell for the sensational Molly Price, aged 18. During a dance, Mary had the opportunity of exerting the full force of her personality on the helpless maiden. She followed this by writing passionate love-letters that completely overwhelmed her, and calling at the Price home to declare her feelings. Molly, trembling with joy, agreed to marry her ardent lover two days later. She was most hurt and indignant when her older sister made slighting remarks about her fiancé's masculinity.

The wedding was celebrated in the time-honoured way, with a handsome bridegroom, blushing bride and proud parents. The newlyweds grew increasingly fond of one another as the weeks sped by. How long this state of affairs would have lasted is a matter of conjecture, but unluckily for Mary, trouble was on the horizon.

One morning she rode to Glastonbury to see a patient, who just happened to have a friend from Totnes staying in the house. The man immediately recognized Mary. Waiting until she had left, he related the story of her scandalous marriage to Miss Ivythorn.

Such news travels fast; it reached Wells before Mary did. Molly's mother questioned her daughter very closely, but although Molly stoutly refused to betray her husband, the woman was suspicious enough to have a constable waiting with a warrant to arrest Mary as she arrived home. She was dragged in front of a magistrate and examined. Poor Molly, distraught with misery at the loss of her partner, fainted clean away. Mary was committed to the Bridewell in Taunton to await trial.

Of course, the outcome of the trial was predictable. Convicting her of the 'base and scandalous crime' of marrying with her own sex, the Court, still in some confusion, sentenced 'her or him, whichever he or she may be', to be imprisoned six months, and, during that time, to be whipped in the towns of Taunton, Glastonbury, Wells and Shepton Mallet.

The severity of the whippings caused great distress to her many admirers as they watched her sufferings. Mary, irrepressible as ever, attempted to bribe the gaoler on the night after her first public beating to procure a young girl in the crowd who had caught her fancy!

Her punishment could have been worse. A similar wrongdoer, Ann Marrow, who also married three of her own sex 30 years later, was put in the public pillory. She was pelted with so many missiles by an infuriated predominantly masculine mob that she was permanently blinded and disfigured.

The Buccaneer Batsman

BY THE side of a country road skirting the Quantock Hills, stood a solitary young man carrying a holdall. He stared anxiously down the empty highway, knowing he had missed the bus. Early on that cold morning of 18th May 1935, there was no traffic, seemingly no possibility of reaching Frome in time. Stoically, he shouldered his bag and strode out. Behind him, he suddenly heard the faint whine of an approaching lorry; he waved hopefully, the driver stopped, and he hopped into the cab. Arriving at Frome he hastily changed into his kit, and, soon afterwards, with a borrowed bat in his hand, walked nervously onto the cricket pitch. Sixty three minutes later, he had scored a century for Somerset, shattering Essex with his sensational hitting and winning the match. It was the most spectacular and electrifying debut in the history of county cricket. The fair haired, muscular, 20 year old hero of the day who achieved this feat was Harold Gimblett from Bicknoller.

Ironically, it was only by the merest fluke that his fairy tale innings happened at all. As a young hopeful on a fortnight's trial for the county, Harold had been brusquely told he was just not good enough, and was about to catch the bus home when he heard the news that one of the team was injured. Incredibly, none of Somerset's many amateurs could be summoned up at a day's notice to play the important match against Essex at Frome. There was no alternative; the only man available was the rejected Gimblett.

When he came in to bat at No 8 on that memorable afternoon, Somerset were facing defeat at the hands of England fast bowler Maurice Nichols. His glorious match-winning innings included three sixes and 17 fours. He had hitch-hiked into the record books, and was awarded the Lawrence Trophy for the fastest century of the season. It proved to be the first of many great occasions for the Somerset farmer's son, who came to be regarded as the most exciting English batsman of his day.

Harold Gimblett was born on 19th October 1914 at Blakes Farm, Bicknoller, the third son of Percy and Louise Gimblett. As he made his entry into the world, the doctor exclaimed at the baby's unusually muscular body. The sturdy infant grew into a well-built lad, whose leisure time was spent playing improvised games of cricket with bat and tennis ball in the orchard with his brothers. His first organized game, when he was nine, at Williton Rec, ended abruptly when young Harold took a swipe at the third ball of the match and whacked it straight into Mr Jones's apple trees, from whence it was never recovered. The first six ever scored by Gimblett and the match was abandoned!

At eleven, Harold was sent off to join his brothers at West Buckland school in North Devon, where he quickly made his presence felt in the First XI. By the time he left school in 1931, his reputation was already marching ahead of him into club cricket, and he was snapped up by Watchet CC. In June 1932, he was invited to play for the Somerset Stragglers against Wellington School. He had a marvellous time: in 75 minutes he scored 142 - his maiden century.

He turned out regularly for Watchet for four seasons, during which time the Club Secretary, W.G. Penny, became convinced that the farm boy had enough talent to be a county player and even an England player. He persuaded and cajoled Somerset officials to give the lad a trial. Eventually, after a great deal of shilly-shallying, they agreed, only to decide he was not good enough. Which is where we came in.

Gimblett played cricket for Somerset from 1935 to 1954. During that time he scored 49 centuries for his county, exceeding 1,000 runs a season twelve times. His highest score was 310 against Sussex at Eastbourne in August 1948. He notched up 23,007 runs in first class cricket, 21,142 of those for Somerset. He played three times for England but the war disrupted his Test career; thousands of county runs would also have been his during those six years. He brought untold pleasure to Somerset's cricket lovers, and was idolized by its school-boys, large numbers of whom would flock to the county ground in St James Street, Taunton, to gaze at him majestically hitting boundaries and demoralizing the bowlers. They adored his buccaneer approach to batting. One day, after his partner had appealed against the light, he promptly hit three sixes.

And yet . . . . despite his success, there was another Gimblett: introspective, moody, irascible, suffering severe bouts of mental illness interspersed with hypochondria. He had an almighty chip on his shoulder, violently resenting the low status of professional cricketers. He despised officials, whom he called 'puffed-up buffoons', and loathed criticism in any shape or form. One indication of his unpredictable behaviour came in 1933, when he was playing for Watchet against the Somerset Stragglers: Harold took just 80 minutes to score 150, and then walked off the pitch. On another occasion, his aggressive feelings for the 'Gentlemen' players came bubbling to the surface as he heard one unwisely boasting that he could bowl 'this blighter' Gimblett out with ease. Harold bided his time at the crease, and when the right ball reached him, let fly with a ferocious shot straight at the head of the boaster, who, flinging up his hands in self-defence, sustained a serious injury.

On bad days, when he felt he had not given of his best, it was quite usual for him to stalk back to the dressing room in a rage and hurl his bat around in self-disgust. The other professionals quickly learnt to beat a hasty retreat when he was upset, not too keen on being on the receiving end of a Gimblett throw. He was certainly a hypochondriac, swallowing all sorts of pills, complaining of headaches, pains in his legs, even giving up his wicket if injured. In 1950, having at last been recalled to the England side after an absence of eleven years for the third Test against the West Indies, he developed a carbuncle on his neck and decided not to play. Years later, this is still remembered by many youngsters of the day as one of cricket's most publicized disappointments. A few days later, he was busily scoring a half century in a county match.

In 1952 came his benefit year. Harold grumbled bitterly and justifiably about the system that called for the beneficiary to defray all the expenses of a match. A fixture at Glastonbury, although well-organized, brought him just over £7. His total benefit was £3,367, not much reward for the amount of pleasure he had given over the years. Compared with the benefits of today's stars it appears niggardly indeed. Geoff Boycott's benefit in 1984 brought in £147,000, and in the same year, Somerset's Ian Botham collected £90,000.

By the end of 1953, Harold's mental health had deteriorated alarmingly. He was unable to sleep, and suffered periods of amnesia. He entered Tone Vale Hospital for 16 weeks to undergo electro-convulsant therapy, which appeared to help him, although the improvement was probably more to do with being in an environment where no demands were made of him. He simply could not cope with the constant pressure of always being expected to excel at the crease. In the first match of the 1954 season he struggled to make 29 runs, returning to the dressing room overcome by wretchedness. The next match, against Yorkshire, was his swan song for Somerset - in a final desperate effort to pull himself together he went bravely to the wicket, but was caught for a duck. Packing his bags, he walked away from county cricket. His final feelings for the Somerset officials were of hatred; he reckoned that they had not appreciated his skill, nor had they supported him during his illness.

Gimblett spent 20 years as an assistant coach at Millfield School, half hoping, despite his animosity, for a recall to county cricket. He still played club cricket, but was increasingly bothered by recurrent back problems. Inevitably, the demons in his head began to take hold once more, and his feelings for Millfield also turned to hatred. He had another dose of electric shock treatment, but the decline continued. On medical advice he decided to retire.

He moved with his wife, Rita, to Minehead, and was

disheartened not to find the serenity he craved. On a whim, soon regretted, the couple left Somerset and bought a mobile home in Verwood, Dorset, on the fringe of Ringwood Forest. Here, too, Harold battled against depression, while enduring increasing pain from arthritis. In an heroic attempt to help people whose mental fragility he understood only too well, he joined the Samaritans. He counselled those in torment, only to find that his own agony was intensifying. He gave willingly of himself until there was nothing left to give. On 30th March 1978, at the age of 63, Harold Gimblett killed himself.

Somerset's greatest home-grown batsman was dead. And yet his records live on. In spite of the wonderful talents of men like Viv Richards and Ian Botham in the Somerset team, three of Gimblett's records remain unbeaten: the most runs (21,142), the most centuries (49), and the most times 1,000 runs in a season (12). He would surely be tickled pink to know that.

Life and Death
on the
Western Circuit

JUDGES of Assize riding the Western Circuit in the 16th and 17th centuries set out from Holborn on horseback, accompanied by a team of clerks and servants, and proceeded from town to town, dispensing justice as they went. They stayed at the homes of local gentry, who took pleasure in entertaining their Lordships as royally as possible. Chard was an important Assize town on the route, and many of the principal folk, eager to show hospitality, presented the convivial lawyers with mouthwatering goodies to expand both menu and waistline. Among the delicious dishes prepared for them were curlew and gull, served with mustard and vinegar sauce, and peacock cooked in wine. Large quantities of capon, lobster, rabbit, salmon, trout, venison, pike and carp were enthusiastically devoured. A favourite tipple was local ale - they emptied a butt (100 gallons!) in five days.

Having refreshed themselves, the Judges got down to the serious business of administering the law. At the Spring Assizes in 1614, they tried Master Babb for the murder of a rich widow from Kingston St Mary, just north of Taunton.

Babb, a very self-satisfied fellow, had proposed marriage to the lady, but to his amazement she turned him down. He stewed about his rejection for a while, and then decided to give her another chance. One evening, he hid himself in her brewhouse and waited for her to come in alone. When she did, she was taken aback, but not alarmed, by his sudden appearance. He blurted out his desire to marry her, but she spurned his offer with great vehemence, crying 'Have thee, base rascal! No!' She then made the mistake of striking at him with a candlestick.

Overcome with rage, Babb seized her, threw her to the ground, and stabbed her 15 times. Three of the wounds were fatal. He stared at the body, frantically trying to think what to do with it. Then he had a brainwave. Thrusting the gory knife into her lifeless hand, he plunged it into the largest gash. Leaving the corpse in a spreading pool of blood, he made his escape.

Shortly afterwards, the woman's servants came to look for their mistress and discovered the horrid deed. To begin with, both they and the coroner were fooled by Babb's ploy; they all assumed the widow had killed herself. The poor woman was subjected to the ritual interment of a suicide - burial at a crossroads at midnight, with a stake driven through the body. But she had a powerful friend, Mr Wane, a Taunton magistrate, who was convinced that she would never have done such a thing. He ordered the corpse to be exhumed and commanded all the inhabitants within a three mile radius to gather beside the grave. An ancient superstition, very firmly believed in those days, held that if a corpse was touched by its murderer, it would bleed, thus pinpointing the killer. All those present were required to undergo the test. Babb, trying to avoid the moment of truth, slid quietly away, but his departure was observed and he was followed. He gave his pursuers the slip, managing to reach a safe haven at his sister's house. However, he was beginning to feel overcome with remorse for his crime; he also felt he was being haunted by the ghost of his victim. He resolved to give himself up.

The Judges of the Western Circuit took very little time over him. He was pronounced guilty and sentenced to death. An eye witness at his execution, Sir Simond D'Ewes, who greatly enjoyed watching malefactors being strung up, described the end of Master Babb. 'He was a handsome proper man; ascended the ladder in mourning apparel, and expressed so many signs of true repentance during his imprisonment, and so much patience and constancy at the time of his suffering, as all that had seen his demeanour there . . . esteemed his soul in a happy condition.'

The Chard Assizes ended, and their Lordships packed up and moved on to Exeter, replete not only with the knowledge that justice had been done, but also with much fine Somerset food and ale.

Lady Elizabeth's Lover

A LITTLE over 400 years ago, a richly dressed young man stood in the doorway of Stogumber church. He was the wealthy and handsome Sir William Courtenay, and he was waiting for the arrival of his bride, Lady Elizabeth of Combe Sydenham. As her carriage drew up at the porch, he stepped forward eagerly to welcome her, but she seemed strangely hesitant about entering the church.

Then all at once, hurtling out of a clear blue sky, a fiery meteorite came crashing to the ground, landing at the very feet of the bride!

Sir William, anxious for her safety, tried to clasp her in his arms, but she, gazing with sparkling eyes at the glowing orb, had her thoughts firmly fixed on another. She *knew* this was a sign from her long-absent true love, the great Sir Francis Drake. Indeed, she thought it must be a cannonball fired from his ship, the *Golden Hind.* Whatever its origins, the alien object put a stop to the wedding, since Elizabeth flatly refused to continue with the ceremony.

The very same iron sphere, weighing over 100 lb and the size of a football, now occupies a place of honour in the Great Hall at Combe Sydenham House, a delightful old place nestling in a wooded valley on the edge of Exmoor, between Wiveliscombe and Watchet. The house and grounds are open to the public from April to October. The estate of Combe was acquired by Richard Sydenham, Justice of the Common Pleas, in 1367, but the present house, originally 'E'-shaped, was built by Sir George Sydenham, a former High Sheriff of Somerset and the father of Lady Elizabeth, in 1580.

At the time of our tale, Francis Drake was already a national hero. He had returned from his three year privateering voyage round the world in 1580, and was enjoying his position as favourite of Queen Elizabeth, who knighted him on board the *Golden Hind.* With some of the vast fortune amassed on his travels he bought the Buckland Abbey estate in Devon, establishing himself as a country gentleman. Alas, his first wife, Mary, had little time to rejoice in her new home. She died just one year later.

Soon afterwards, Sir Francis, then 40, met the beautiful Elizabeth Sydenham at Court, and promptly lost his heart to her. She returned his love, being irresistibly attracted to this man 'of strong limbs, broad breasted, round headed, brown hayre, full bearded, his eyes round, large and cleare, well favored, fayre, and of a cheerefull countenance'.

Unfortunately for the lovers, her father did not approve her choice. Sir George, conscious of his impeccable lineage stretching back to the Norman Conquest, looked upon Sir Francis as a conceited, middle aged, jumped-up sailor, who was certainly no gentleman. He wished his heiress daughter to marry his own great friend, Sir William Courtenay of Powderham Castle. Elizabeth resisted the match and, in the teeth of parental opposition, determined to wed her bold seaman.

According to legend, Sir Francis made his sweetheart promise to be faithful during his frequent enforced absences on naval business, and swore that if she favoured another suitor he would somehow come between them. He is said to have sailed away on a hazardous mission, and that no news of his whereabouts was received by the lonely girl. Amusingly enough, the years between 1582 and 1585 actually seem singularly devoid of seafaring exploits for Drake - he spent most of the time either in London or Plymouth!

Sir George took advantage of his disappearance to encourage the ever-devoted Sir William to woo Elizabeth once more. Convinced by her family that Francis was dead, she at last agreed to the marriage. The wedding day dawned; bride and groom, accompanied by many friends, made their separate ways to the magnificent church at Stogumber, two miles from Combe Sydenham. William, arriving first, waited impatiently; Elizabeth, her heart still Drake's, came more slowly, praying that even now he might send word to her. The dramatic arrival of the thunderbolt cast Drake as a Zeus-like figure in her eyes. Her father and her bridegroom tried to persuade her to go on with the wedding, but she was now confident that her missing lover was on his way to claim her.

Shortly afterwards, he did indeed arrive hotfoot from Plymouth, and with little delay the couple were married on 8th February 1585. By August, Elizabeth was alone again as her dashing husband set sail from Plymouth in the *Elizabeth Bonaventure* to continue ' the singeing of the King of Spain's beard' with a successful raid on the

Spanish West Indies. In all, the pair had eleven years of happiness together, during which time Drake became England's greatest hero at the defeat of the Armada in 1588. He died at sea on 28th January 1596. In his will he left 'to Dame Elizabeth, my wife, all my furniture, goods, implements and household stuff whatsoever standing and being within the doors of my mansion and the land and house of Buckland Abbey.' But the item that she prized above all was the strange cannonball that had proved such a forceful token of his desire for her.

Legend assures us that if Drake's cannonball is ever moved from its rightful place in the hall at Combe Sydenham it will return of its own volition. It was taken from the house some years ago, to be displayed in Taunton Museum, but it is back in position now, regarded by many as an object of great good fortune.

If you have a sneaking sympathy for the jilted would-be husband Sir William Courtenay, you might be pleased to know that he did, at last, attain his heart's desire; he married the widowed Lady Drake in 1597.

To The
Manor Born

IF YOU are one of the many thousands who have visited Cricket St Thomas Wildlife Park, just off the A30 between Crewkerne and Chard, you will have discovered the amazing variety of animals and birds, from elephants to emus, which roam the grounds. You may also be aware that the immensely popular TV series *To the Manor Born* was filmed on location at Cricket. But you may not know that Cricket House has a fascinating history of its own. Its occupants, though perhaps less exotic than the golden-headed quetzal, red-bellied tamarin or Penelope Keith and Peter Bowles, have certainly been as remarkable, including an Elizabethan pirate, a naval hero and Big Fry himself - boss of the chocolate-making firm of J.S. Fry & Sons.

Tucked away in rolling South Somerset countryside, Cricket St Thomas House ('cric' was once the word for ridge, St Thomas comes from the name of the nearby church) is sheltered by hills on three sides. The northern boundary of the 1,000 acre estate is the aptly named Windwhistle Hill from which, on a clear day, you can see the Bristol Channel to the north and the cliffs at Beer in Devon to the south. The hill, at night a wild and lonely place, was a favourite haunt of highwaymen in the 18th century. The old Roman road along its ridge was a busy coaching route between London and Exeter, providing ample opportunity for gentlemen of the road to relieve travellers of their valuables before melting away into the safety of the beech trees adorning the ridge.

The land slopes from 750 ft at the top of Windwhistle Hill down 300 ft to the banks of the Purtington stream, a small tributary of the river Axe, which flows through the valley below the house. This delightful position was glowingly described in a Victorian sale catalogue: 'It would be difficult . . . . to over-rate the beauties of this estate and the country by which it is surrounded. The pure and salubrious air of the property and all round about it, has made well known that it is one of the healthiest places in the United Kingdom.'

The first mention of a manor house on the estate was in 1313. The tenants at that time were the de Crickets, the family taking its name from the land. In 1328-9 Michael de Cricket sold the manor to Sir Walter de Rodney, an ancester of the celebrated admiral Lord George Rodney. By 1466, it had passed into the hands of Stephen and Maud Preston, whose heirs lived at Cricket for the next three centuries. It was one of this family, Amyas Preston, who became an Elizabethan pirate.

The date of his birth is unknown, but he was married to Julian Burye in 1581. Four years later, on a profitable privateering voyage, he captured a Portuguese ship and brought it safely home to England. His prowess both as mariner and as leader served his country well when the Spanish Armada arrived in the Channel. He was lieutenant of the flagship *Ark*, and commanded the longboats in the daring attack on the largest of the four galleons which was stranded outside Calais. Hugo de Moncada, its captain, was killed in the fierce hand-to-hand fighting along with many of his crew. Most of the rest jumped overboard, leaving our wounded hero to free the 300 wretched slaves who manned the oars and then rifle the ship with his comrades.

The following year, successful pirating in the Azores in his own vessel, *Julian,* (named for his wife) brought him prize money of £30,000. In 1596, as captain of the *Ark* during the Cadiz expedition, he was knighted by Admiral Lord Howard.

He had a stormy relationship with another West Country seaman - Sir Walter Raleigh. There was a long-standing dispute between them over some prize money, and eventually, in 1601, although Raleigh was a Privy Councillor and far above him in status, Amyas issued a challenge. Raleigh did not bother to answer so the affair fizzled out. From 1603 until his death in 1617 Sir Amyas Preston, ex-pirate, held the office of Keeper of Stores and Ordnance in the Tower.

A descendant of this bold adventurer sold the family seat for £14,000 in 1775. The buyer was Captain Alexander Hood RN. Around this time, Cricket House was either burnt down or demolished, and a new building erected some 200 yards south of the former site. Hood commissioned one of England's leading architects, Sir John Soane, to enlarge and alter the new house. Soane added bedrooms, dining room, servants' hall, plus a complete wing. While all these modifications were in progress, Hood was making rapid strides in his naval career. On the outbreak of war with France in 1793, as Vice-Admiral Sir Alexander Hood KCB, he became second-in-command of the Channel Fleet under Earl Howe. In 1794, for his distinguished service in the operations ending with the great sea battle known as the

'Glorious First of June' in which six French ships were captured, he was created Baron Bridport of Cricket St Thomas. His deeds were immortalized in a stirring naval ballad.

Now, my brave boys, down Channel we steer
'Long with brave Bridport in search of Mounseer.
May Heaven but grant what we crave for a boon,
That these boasting invaders may out to us come,
And the tune that we will play them is the 'First of June'.

After the Spithead mutiny of 1797, he took the fleet to sea as commander-in-chief, personally directing the blockade of Brest from 1798-1800. On his retirement he was created Viscount Bridport. Although twice married, he died childless in 1814 at the venerable age of 87, and lies buried in Cricket church. His monument records his achievements: 'Admiral of the Red Squadron of His Majesty's Fleet, Vice-Admiral of Great Britain, General of the Main Forces, and the Senior Admiral of the Royal Navy'.

The estate and the barony went to his great-nephew, Samuel, already married to Charlotte Nelson, niece of Admiral Lord Nelson. The new Lord Bridport set about his own alterations - not to the house, but to the land around it. The Purtington stream was dammed, forming a three-quarter mile chain of lakes separated by waterfalls. He came to the conclusion that the view from the house was spoilt by the motley collection of villagers' cottages on the west bank of the stream, and decided to get rid of them, rehousing the occupants out of sight. In this, he was following the example of other West Country landowners such as the Trevelyans of Nettlecombe Court and Joseph Damer of Milton Abbas. By 1851, only two dwellings remained, one of them belonging to the gamekeeper. The 69 residents of the parish were all employed on estate work, except for a shoemaker and a woman glover. The Baron closed the roads and footpaths in the middle of his domain to public use, turning the whole area into a park, and carrying out an extensive tree planting programme to beautify his 16 acres of garden.

Lord Bridport died in 1868 and was succeeded by his eldest son, Alexander Nelson Hood. In spite of his name, he chose to enter the Army rather than the Navy and did well - he rose to the rank of General. He held positions at Court, spending much time at Windsor. When in residence at Cricket House he entertained lavishly and with style. He was the last member of the illustrious Hood family to live there; he sold the estate, encumbered with mortgages, in 1897.

The new lord of the manor of Cricket St Thomas was neither soldier nor seaman, but an extremely prosperous businessman - Francis James Fry, the chocolate manufacturer. Aged 62 when he moved into the house, he thought it could do with some changes. Unlike previous owners he chose to demolish instead of construct, removing the conservatories and, sadly, all of Sir John Soane's interior decoration of library and drawing room. He lived in the house until his death in 1918.

Of the subsequent owners of Cricket House, the most influential were the Taylor family, occupants until 1998. In 1967 they opened Cricket St Thomas to the public as a Wildlife Park and their success has led to great expansion. One day is hardly enough to enjoy all that is on offer, from the lemurs wandering freely and safely in the lakeside woods to the rare and spectacular Amur leopards. Those creatures of a more cuddly and docile disposition such as rabbits and guinea pigs can be petted by young visitors at Pets Corner. But cute though these small animals are, it is the conservation of some of the planet's endangered species that is the worthy aim of the new owners of Cricket St Thomas.

If the ghost of Samuel Hood were to revisit his old haunts just over a century later, he would be delighted with the sight of the mature cedars, cypresses and wellingtonias which he planted to enhance his property, but perplexed, yet enchanted, by the strange assortment of exotic birds and beasts taking their ease beside the lakes he created.

Witches'
Brew

B ELIEF in witches was once so widespread in England that 30,000 people were put to death in the space of 200 years. Most of them were harmless old women living alone, who were persecuted by the superstitious and executed by the unjust. The last judicial murder took place in 1716, but, as late as 1730, in Frome, an aged crone suspected of being a witch was forced to undergo the ordeal by water, watched by 200 taunting, cheering spectators. Half-drowned during the process, she was finally dragged from the millpond and dumped in a stable, where she died about an hour later.

When not airborne, witches were particularly thick on the ground in Somerset. One of the most interesting, Jane Brooks, lived in Shepton Mallet. She was denounced for bewitching a twelve year old boy, Richard Jones. He claimed that one morning in November, 1657, she came to his home, where he happened to be on his own, and offered him an apple. The lad cooked the apple, ate it, and immediately fell violently ill. His father decided that the sickness was caused by Jane's evil powers, and she was brought before two magistrates, Mr Carey and Mr Hunt at Castle Cary on 8th December. As soon as the boy began

his testimony, Jane stared fixedly at him, at which he lost the ability to speak. He remained dumb until she was taken from the room. Since no other evidence was offered, she was set free. But more serious accusations were soon laid against her, and she was imprisoned to await trial.

At the Chard Assizes in March 1658 she was tried for witchcraft by Sir John Glyn. Several witnesses claimed that Richard was often to be heard making strange noises like the croakings of a toad, an animal generally associated with the black arts, which repeated the name 'Jane Brooks' over and over. One woman insisted that she had seen the boy rise up from the ground in front of her eyes, ascending higher and higher so that he was lifted over the garden wall and swept along for about 300 yards, eventually crashing to earth at the front door of a Mr Jordan, where he lay as if dead for some time. When he recovered his senses, he told the woman that Jane Brooks had taken him up by the arms and flown with him through the air.

Another witness swore that Richard had been found 'strangely hanging above the ground with his hands flat against the sides of a great beam in the top of the room and all his body two or three feet from the ground, and hath so remained a quarter of an hour at a time'. Nine other people agreed that they had seen the phenomenon.

Such damning evidence being impossible to disprove, Jane Brooks was found guilty of witchcraft and hanged on 26th March 1658.

A famous witch from West Somerset was Mother Shipton, renowned especially as a prophetess. She is connected particularly with the area around Williton and Watchet. Her mother, Agatha, was also supposed to be a witch, so when she gave birth to a daughter, Ursula, in 1472, the baby was labelled the 'Devil's child' by fearful neighbours. Unfortunately, Ursula was incredibly ugly, with crooked limbs and huge protruberant eyes. Nevertheless, when she was in her early 20s she managed to catch herself a husband, Tobias Shipton. She made dozens of prophecies, some of which are still remembered today. She foretold flooding on a disastrous scale affecting ports in the Bristol Channel. She warned that Porlock would be under water, and that ships would use the spire at St Dubricius' church as a mooring post. She also claimed that

> Watchet and Doniford both shall drown
> And Williton become the seaport town

Luckily, neither of these forecasts came true. Nor did the one that predicted the end of the world on Good Friday, 1881, beginning with an earthquake at Ham Hill, near Yeovil!

She died in 1561, but her sayings were collected in a pamphlet published 80 years later. She is supposed to have been buried near Williton, and indeed there is a strange stone in the woods between Nettlecombe and Williton, bearing a Latin inscription, and popularly known as 'Mother Shipton's Tomb'. Sadly, this stone was revealed as a fake in 1879. It is a copy of a Roman burial stone, recording the death of a young girl, Julia Martima, aged twelve years, three months, 22 days. Whether Mother Shipton is interred anywhere nearby will remain forever a mystery.

Joan Carne seems to have had *two* final resting-places: the first in a church, the second in a pond! She lived at Sandhill Farm (still standing), near Withycombe. She aroused the suspicions of people in the vicinity because of the speed with which she married and buried three husbands. The first was John Newton, the tenant of Sandhill Farm, whom she wed in 1573. After his demise she chose Charles Wyndham, from nearby Orchard Wyndham. He soon followed his predecessor to the grave, to be promptly replaced by Thomas Carne, a Welshman. His luck was no better than the others; Joan was shortly donning her widow's weeds again.

By now, the locals were convinced that she was a sorceress, who had disposed of her menfolk by vile means. They credited her with the power of being able to turn herself into a hare, as all proper witches can. On one occasion, when she was apparently thus transformed, she was grabbed and struck over the head, before managing to escape. Next day, she was wearing a bandage on her head, which proved to everyone's satisfaction that she was indeed a witch.

When she died on 29th October 1612, there was general rejoicing. She was buried in Withycombe church, where her memorial brass can still be seen over the choir stalls. It reads

'Here lyeth the bodie of Joane Carne, of Sandell, who was thrice married; first unto John Newton of Sandell, gent.; next unto Charles Wyndham Esquire; and last of all unto Thomas Carne of Eweny, in the county of Glamorgan, Esquire. She died on the nine and twentieth day of October 1612.'

After she had ostensibly been laid to rest, the mourners returned to the house at Sandhill and were understandably terrified to find her busily cooking bacon and eggs in the kitchen! Not content with culinary exploits, Joan

57

haunted her old home for months, roaming through the house, dislodging the furniture and frightening the servants.

At last, it was agreed that the only way to get rid of the old hag was to exorcise her. The villagers turned out in force to witness the ceremony, conducted by the parson from Watchet, carrying bell, book and candle. Joan's ghost was solemnly laid in a stagnant pond, in a field down Sandhill Lane, known ever since as the Witch's Pool. She is thought to be making her way, at a cockstride (five or six inches) a year, back to her old home. When she arrives, Sandhill Farm will go up in flames, they say. However, the present owner, who feels the house holds no malevolent memories, does not seem at all worried by the prospect of her return!

The
Taunton
Maidens

TALES OF Sedgemoor and the Duke of Monmouth are legion. Many are tragic, some grisly, a few ghostly. None is particularly light-hearted, since death, slavery or ruin was the fate of those who rebelled against King James II. Nevertheless, the story of the Taunton Maidens does have a pretty beginning, although its sequel is not so pretty.

The Maidens were schoolgirls aged eight to 16, daughters of the most prosperous merchants in Taunton, all pupils at an exclusive seminary for young ladies. On 18th June 1685, their hearts were a-flutter at the news of the arrival of the handsome and dashing James Scott, Duke of Monmouth, with his army of rebels. The Duke had been in England exactly a week, landing at Lyme Regis on 11th June. Since then, he had been attracting large numbers of recruits from among the ordinary West Country folk as he marched towards Taunton to make his headquarters there.

The good people of the town, many of them violently anti-Catholic, were delighted to welcome the Protestant

Duke with his 4,000 followers, and tried to outdo each other with the warmth of their reception. The streets through which he rode were strewn with flowers, and at every window waving, cheering spectators, overcome with the emotion of the moment, shouted 'A Monmouth! A Monmouth!' Doors and windowsills were decorated with green branches, flowers and herbs, and almost every hat wore a green sprig, a token of support for the Duke.

The schoolgirls, caught up in romantic daydreams, determined to proffer a special gift to their hero. Silk petticoats were cheerfully surrendered to provide the material for 27 decorated banners for the Duke's regiments. The following morning the girls, carrying their flags, marched behind their teachers, Mary Blake and Susannah Musgrave, to the Duke's lodgings. He was staying with Captain John Hucker, a wealthy serge merchant, who lived in East Street just about where the County Hotel is now. Monmouth was greatly flattered by the open adoration of so many young ladies. He was presented first of all with a Bible by Mary Blake, and then the maidens stepped forward one by one to bestow their banners. Each blushing cheek received a kiss in payment. Last in line was the oldest pupil, Mary Mead, whose intricately embroidered flag bore his initials surmounted by a crown.

Believing that the people of Taunton wished him to be England's monarch, Monmouth at last made the decision to have himself proclaimed King. This final act of rebellion against James II took place next day at the Market Cross. No doubt the Taunton Maidens were part of the enthusiastic crowd which heard and applauded the Proclamation. The following morning, 'King' Monmouth, with 6,000 troops, left Taunton for Bridgwater.

Less than a month later he was dead, messily butchered on Tower Hill by the notorious Jack Ketch. His friends in Somerset were left to face the fury of King James in the person of George Jeffreys, Lord Chief Justice of England.

Jeffreys arrived in Taunton on 17th September. It was Somerset's turn for the 'Bloody Assizes'. During the next two days, he and four colleagues sat in the Great Hall in Taunton Castle and decided the fate of more than 500 wretched prisoners. The Taunton Maidens were subjected to Jeffrey's fierce questioning. One little girl stammered out a plea for mercy, but instead of softening his heart, she was singled out for a torrent of abuse which so terrified her that she collapsed on the floor in a heap, tying to hide from him by pulling her hood over her face. Jeffreys ordered her removal from his Court and, weeping piteously, she was carried out by a jailer. The poor child did not recover from the shock of her experience and died the same day.

The rest of the girls were 'given' to the Queen's Maids of Honour. This meant that the children's parents were forced to pay a ransom to these ladies to secure their freedom. It was an effective and much-used method of rewarding friends while punishing enemies. The original total sum demanded was £8,000 - about £250 a girl. However, negotiations dragged on for such a time that the girls had to be excluded from the General Pardon of March 1686, because otherwise the Maids of Honour would have been denied their present. Agreement was finally reached on a figure of about £100 each, and the Taunton Maidens were returned to their families.

Mary Blake, the school mistress who had led the procession, escaped from Taunton but was later captured and thrown into Dorchester Gaol. In this noisome, overcrowded dungeon she contracted

61

smallpox, which was rife among the prisoners, and died on 25th November.

The other teacher, Susannah Musgrave, had also managed to evade arrest, and spent several months in hiding on Exmoor, sheltered by a Nonconformist minister, Joseph Chadwick, and his wife. In May 1686, she was enjoying a meal in Dulverton with the Chadwicks and other friends when the local constable arrived to take her into custody. The Chadwicks, however, stoutly refused to give her up, soundly berating the poor man for being part of such a sorry business. Overwhelmed by their forcefulness, he decided that discretion was the better part of valour and left them in peace. No further attempts were made to arrest her. She was one of the lucky ones.

Captain John Hucker, Monmouth's jovial host in Taunton, at whose house the Maidens presented the colours, was less fortunate: Jeffreys sentenced him to death, and on 30th September 1685 he was hanged. His property was confiscated and bestowed on the Devon-born man who was second-in-command of the Royal Army — Major-General Lord John Churchill, later the first Duke of Marlborough.

The Wizard
of The Quantocks

H IGH UP in the Quantocks, with spectacular views
over the Bristol Channel, sits the tranquil little
village of Broomfield. On its fringe is the manor of Fyne
Court, which is a lovely place to visit, with 24 acres of
woods, lakes and varied wildlife including badgers and
kingfishers. Since 1974 the estate has been the home of
the Somerset Trust for Nature Conservancy. Although
Fyne Court was almost completely destroyed by fire in
1898, those parts left standing - a wing containing a music
room and laboratory, and the coach house - are now used
as a base for nature studies. What could be more peaceful
than a stroll along the nature trails in the grounds or a
browse among the fascinating exhibits in the meeting
room? Yet, 150 years ago, people believed that devils
roamed the grounds and that black magic was practised
in that same laboratory by a malevolent wizard! Flashes
of lightning and ear-splitting bangs shattered the quiet
countryside, terrifying the villagers. A clergyman from
Bridgwater came to conduct a service of exorcism on a
nearby hill to drive out the demons.

The cause of all this consternation was Andrew Crosse,
a man who, but for an over whelming passion for

electrical science, would probably have been a benign squire beloved by his tenants instead of their unwitting tormentor. He was born at Fyne Court on 17th June 1784, the elder son of Richard and Susannah Crosse. He was sent to school in Bristol in 1793, where his obsession for the infant science of electricity was sparked off by the progressive headmaster, Dr Samuel Seyer. His early experiments with a home-made 'electrifying machine' were not appreciated by schoolfellows on the receiving end of painful surprises.

When he was 16, his father died and he inherited the family estate. His mother sent him to Brasenose College, Oxford, which he loathed, describing it as a 'perfect hell upon earth'. Her death in 1805 proved a terrible blow, and for a while he and his brother Richard went off the rails, holding extravagant house parties. Then he met George Singer, two years his junior but already regarded as a brilliant electrical chemist, who inspired him to return to his experiments.

During the next few years, as well as finding a wife and fathering seven children, he was engrossed in pioneering research into electricity and the elements. The inhabitants of Broomfield gazed in open-mouthed bewilderment as a mile of copper wire was strung on poles round the trees at his home, enabling Crosse to conduct lightning into the laboratory. He built a large electrical battery which could be charged and discharged 20 times a minute with the electricity collected from the wire. This process produced the tumultuous noises that so petrified the locals. Fearfully, they dubbed him the 'thunder and lightning man' and did their utmost to avoid him. Those brave enough to venture anywhere near his house at night reported seeing 'devils all surrounded by lightning, dancing on the wires'.

Trying to ignore both increasing hostility from the villagers and severe financial troubles brought on by the vast sums he poured out on equipment, Crosse immersed himself in his work. By 1822, he had built a huge voltaic battery of 1,025 pairs of metallic plates. News of his extraordinary doings aroused great interest among other scientists, some of whom managed to gain an invitation to the laboratory for an exciting demonstration of the apparatus. The most famous of these visitors was Sir Humphry Davy, who in 1827, although already fatally ill, was determined to meet his fellow West Countryman. And the bangings and crashings increased, wrecking the sleep of the godly and ungodly alike. Blame for a potato blight that ruined the crop in Somerset and Devon was laid at Crosse's door.

The climax to his experiments came in 1837 and was unforeseen, unexpected, utterly astounding. For , inadvertently, he succeeded in doing what scientists had dreamt about for centuries but never accomplished - he created life! He had been following his usual method of producing crystals by passing electricity through different solutions. He was hoping to make crystals of silica grow on an electrified stone, but for two weeks nothing happened. On the 14th day he noticed small white growths on the stone, which continued to develop until by the 26th day each had assumed the form of a perfect insect. A few days later, when Crosse entered his laboratory, he was flabbergasted to see that some had left the stone and were moving around freely. Soon there were more than a hundred of the creatures scuttling about in their enclosure. Suspecting that insect ova had been present in the atmosphere, he repeated the experiment under more stringent conditions. He achieved the same result - more insects appeared, fed, reproduced, and died when the weather turned cold. Quite by chance, it seemed he had cracked the secret of life!

He decided to publicize the results by sending a detailed report to the newly-founded Electrical Society in London. But once the newspapers got hold of the story, a storm of invective poured in from all sides, accusing him of being an atheist, a blasphemer and a 'reviler of our holy religion'. The poor electrician was in despair, unable to comprehend why he had 'met with so much virulence and abuse'.

One great man came to his aid - Michael Faraday - who urged a fair hearing for Crosse and an immediate invest-igation into the amazing appearance of the insects, which he suggested should be named *Acari Crossii*. But the reclusive Somerset man, loathing the publicity, re-treated to his laboratory, hoping the furore would die down. The service of exorcism by the Rev Philip Smith, taking place within earshot of the house, was a deliberate attempt to drive 'Devil' Crosse from his home. This was almost successful, since he would have left England had it not been for his wife's failing health.

After her death, he could not bear to stay in Somerset any longer, and went to London, where Fate, for once, smiled kindly on him in the shape of Cornelia Burns, who was to become his second wife. She fell in love with a man who was greatly misunderstood by the general public. Their first encounter had a tremendous effect on her: 'I had expected to find what I reverenced - a follower of science: I found what I worshipped - a poet'. They were married in London in 1850 and then returned to Fyne Court. The Broomfield villagers, although still wary of him, were no longer plagued by visions of diabolic creatures on the loose, and he was left in peace.

The couple had five years of happiness before the old

scientist died on 6th July 1855. He was buried three days later in Broomfield churchyard. His only memorial is the obelisk on his tomb in a lonely corner of the graveyard, which bears the following inscription:

Sacred
to the memory of
ANDREW CROSSE
The Electrician
Born June 17th 1784
Died July 6th 1855
He was humble towards
God and kind to
his fellow creatures

But there is a curious postscript to the life of Andrew Crosse. On a rare, brief visit to London in 1814, he gave a lecture to a spellbound audience which included the poet Shelley and his future wife, Mary Godwin. Four years later her novel *Frankenstein,* the world's most famous horror story, was published. It could be that, mesmerized by the scientist's manifest obsession with electricity, she used him as her model for Victor Frankenstein. Crosse was certainly the star of two lesser-known works of fiction - *The Electric Vampire* (1910) and *The Thunder and Lightning Man* (1968).

Many theories have been advanced over the years to try to explain Crosse's sensational experiments with the insects. Nobody knows how it was done. If he *did* discover a way of creating life out of a stone, the secret lies buried in Broomfield churchyard.

The Incredible Journey

ONE stormy winter's night, a team of 20 men and as many horses came stumbling and slithering over the summit of Porlock Hill. Before them lay a treacherous, twisting 1,350 foot descent that even in summertime can still alarm the traveller. Sodden, exhausted and battling against time, they were attempting one of history's unique rescue bids. They had already covered ten miles across Exmoor, hauling a $3\frac{1}{2}$ ton, 34 foot lifeboat.

This epic tale began on the evening of 12th January 1899, when the landlord of the Anchor Hotel at Porlock Weir spotted distress signals from a large ship, the *Forrest Hall* of Liverpool, which was drifting helplessly in Porlock Bay. He hurriedly sent a telegram requesting assistance to Tom Bevan, the Lifeboat Secretary at the Lynmouth station. In normal weather the lifeboat would have been launched from Lynmouth and gone east along the coast to Porlock, but with a full northwesterly gale blowing and a turning tide, it was plainly impossible. The boat's coxswain, Jack Crocombe, racking his brains for a solution, came up with an astonishing idea. He suggested that a team of horses could drag the boat on her carriage up the steep incline of Countisbury Hill, across Exmoor and down Porlock Hill, so that she could be launched from a more sheltered beach. His stout-hearted crew were eager to try, but, without the unstinting support of the Lynmouth villagers, they could never have succeeded.

One fellow dashed up the hill to the nearby village of Lynton to beg for horses. He returned in triumph with 20 sturdy horses and the terrific added bonus of Tom Willis, a famous coachman of the day, to handle them. Meanwhile an advance party with shovels, pickaxes and other tools, went on ahead to smooth the path for the lifeboat by demolishing any obvious obstructions in her way. Back in the village, men, women and children toiled in the pouring rain to load the unwieldy craft, named the *Louisa* onto her massive carriage.

At eight o'clock, just one hour after receiving the telegram from Porlock, the *Louisa* was ready. In utter darkness, with only oil lamps to light the way, humans and horses began their backbreaking labour. The road was extremely slippery, and the horses, straining in their harness, skidded in the mud, but somehow, with the shouts of encouragement and extra muscle power of a hundred villagers pushing and pulling, they reached the top of Countisbury Hill. Heaving sighs of relief the party stopped to catch their breath, but, almost as soon as they started off again, disaster struck. One of the carriage wheels, having been constantly jolted and scraped on the edge of the road, fell off. With great difficulty it was refitted. Many of the volunteers, completely worn out and soaked to the skin, were forced to give up and reluctantly trudged home, but the lifeboat crew plus a handful of other stalwarts pressed to go on.

Soon they caught up with the advance party, faced with a narrow lane quite impossible for the *Louisa* to negotiate on her carriage. Undaunted, the men shifted her onto wooden skids, and, while horses and carriage detoured across the heather-covered moorland, pushed the boat forward six feet at a time, with the skids continually shuffled from the back of the boat to the front as she was propelled onward, until the road was wide enough for the carriage to rejoin it. At County Gate, as the *Louisa* crossed into Somerset, a huge gatepost was ripped out to make way for her.

Now the most frightening and hazardous part of the journey was facing them - Porlock Hill! Surely every motorist about to drive down it for the first time, even in the relative safety and comfort of his car, experiences a sensation of stomach-churning nervousness as he engages bottom gear. Every member of the crew must have told himself that he was stark staring mad to contemplate such a descent. As the *Louisa* began to slide down the hill, men and horses fought to hold her back with drag chains and wedges. Tom Willis, hanging on for grim death, somehow managed to control the team on the appalling hairpin bends. Miraculously, they reached the bottom of the hill without mishap, still in command of the boat.

Arriving in Porlock village, a new barrier confronted them - the stone wall of a cottage jutting into the lane. Resolutely, the men set about demolishing the wall, to the fury and consternation of its elderly occupant, startled out of sleep by the thumping of pickaxes under her window. With remarkable composure, as soon as she learnt of the rescue mission on which the crew was bent, she readily allowed the destruction to continue, gazing awestruck at the boat on wheels.

Once past the diminished cottage, the men

71

discovered, with sinking hearts, that the main road to Porlock Weir had been washed away in the storm, so another gigantic effort was required to manoeuvre the *Louisa* onto a higher path. Frustratingly, this way was blocked by the branches of a fallen laburnum tree. One of the men, armed with a saw, doggedly cut through the tangle while the rest cleared the timber from the road.

At six o'clock in the morning, after ten hours of the most gruelling effort, they reached the beach. Without pausing for rest or food, the 13 members of the *Louisa's* crew immediately launched her. For 90 minutes they struggled against huge waves until they made contact with the stricken vessel. They found that the *Forrest Hall*, a fully rigged iron ship of 2,000 tons, had been on tow from Bristol to Liverpool when her towline had parted during the gale. The tug, the *Jane Joliffe*, collided with her, causing such damage to the rudder that the *Forrest Hall*, with no more than a skeleton crew aboard, could only drift powerlessly shorewards, while the tug returned to port for urgent repairs.

At this moment the *Jane Joliffe* reappeared on the scene, and the lifeboatmen successfully passed a line from tug to ship. Some of the men boarded the *Forrest Hall* to assist her crew, while the rest stood by in the *Louisa.* The weather, which had improved a little as dawn broke, suddenly deteriorated, and the towline parted again. The laborious process of passing the line had to be repeated, but, at last, the *Forrest Hall*, with an augmented crew of lifeboatmen, was towed out of the bay, eventually reaching safe anchorage in Barry, Wales, at six o'clock in the evening. After 24 hours of unceasing killing effort, the *Louisa's* crew were cared for by members of the Shipwrecked Mariners Society, who offered them food, dry clothing and beds. Next day, boat and crew arrived home in Lynmouth to a great welcome, having been towed part of the way by a steamer.

Every member of the lifeboat was awarded £5 in recognition of his courage. A Lynmouth resident, R.H. Fry, presented each man with a solid silver watch. The cost of repairs to walls and fences demolished in the course of the *Louisa*'s extraordinary journey, and the hire of the 20 horses totalled £118 17s 9d, to which the owners of the *Forrest Hall* contributed £75. The names of the men who sweated and struggled so heroically will never be forgotten. They are Jack Crocombe (coxswain), George Richards (second coxswain), Richard Ridler (bowman), John Ridler, Richard Burgess, George Rawle, John Ward, William Jarvis, Charles Crick, Bertram Pennicott, David Crocombe, Tom Pugsley and William Richards. The last named was a lad of 16 on his first mission. He went on to play a part in saving the lives of 56 people during his years with the lifeboat crew.

The *Louisa* was withdrawn from service in 1906 and broken up. The *Forrest Hall*, carrying a cargo of coal from Australia to Chile, was lost off the coast of Auckland, New Zealand, in 1909.

Buried
Alive!

I F THE thought of being buried alive sends a shiver down your spine, you would have sympathised with Hans Christian Andersen, who was so tormented by the fear of it that he used to prop a notice by his bedside saying 'I am not really dead.' He also implored his friends to cut one of his arteries to make absolutely sure he had expired before his coffin lid was nailed down. Horror stories with this theme are legion, but two Somerset women really did suffer the experience of premature interment; one survived it and one did not.

The first woman was Lady Florence Wyndham, who lived with her husband, Sir John, at Kentsford Manor, just quarter of a mile from the 15th century church of St Decuman, at Watchet. In the year 1562, she had been married for only two years when she fell ill, lapsed into a coma and was pronounced dead. Mourned by her grief stricken husband and family, she was buried in the family vault in St Peter's chapel on the north side of St Decuman's. Late that same night, however, the sexton (a man called Attewell) came creeping into the dark church.

He knew she was wearing valuable rings, and greed overcame fear as he determined to steal the jewels. He lit

75

a lantern and managed to prise open the leaden lid of the coffin. He struggled to remove some of the rings from Florence's icy hands, but the most dazzling refused to yield to his grasp. Heart beating furiously, and desperate to be gone, he tried to sever the finger with a file. All at once, to his great terror, the 'corpse' moaned, stirred, tried to sit up and screamed for help. Hair standing on end, Attewell panicked and raced from the church. He rushed headlong down St Decuman's Hill, fell into the sea and drowned. Swift justice indeed!

Meanwhile, the resurrected Lady Florence, clutching the sexton's lantern, clad only in her shroud and with blood oozing from her cut hand, made her way shakily down the hill. She crossed the little two-arched packhorse bridge over the Washford stream, passed the weeping ash and mulberry trees, and at last reached her home. She banged at the door for admittance, but Sir John, lying sleepless and distressed in his room, was reluctant to see who dared disturb him. As the knocking continued, he rose angrily, ran down the stairs and flung open the door. The shock of seeing his wife, looking exactly like a ghost, almost unhinged him, but throwing herself into his arms Florence was able to convince him of her reality. Tears of joy were shed by them both as the long dreadful night was transformed into a beautiful dawn. Her recovery was rapid and she soon afterwards gave birth to a healthy son, John. She lived a full and happy life for another 34 years, dying in 1596.

There are portraits of Lady Florence and Sir John, in full Elizabethan dress, chatting to each other, on the fine memorial brasses put up by their son John in the north aisle of St Decuman's.

Eleanor Lovell was not as lucky as Lady Florence. Her high spirits on her wedding day brought about the most terrible tragedy.

76

On a summer's day in 1681, Eleanor was the centre of attention in the village of Bawdrip, near Bridgwater, for she was going to be married in the parish church of St Michael and All Angels, where her father, Edward Lovell, was rector. The bridegroom, also a member of the influential Lovell family from Castle Cary, waited impatiently for his beautiful bride to join him in the church. The wedding ceremony took place amid general rejoicing and was followed by the usual grand post-nuptial festivities.

It was Eleanor herself who suggested a game of hide-and-seek to the younger guests, and she ran off to find a good hiding place in the old rectory with its six foot thick walls and maze of rooms. She spied an ancient oak chest half hidden in the corner of an unused chamber, climbed into it and pulled down the lid. Perhaps she laughed to herself as she imagined her friends hunting for her, no doubt hoping that her husband would be the one to discover her. She waited, and waited, but she had chosen too clever a spot. As time went by and nobody came, the increasing stuffiness in the chest made her anxious to escape.

She tried to raise the heavy lid, but it proved quite beyond her. She cried frantically for help, but her screams, muffled by the thickness of the timber, went unheeded. She could not know of the frenzied search that went on for days and nights, until her distraught husband and family finally gave her up for dead. Her pathetic remains, still in wedding finery, were not revealed till many years later.

Eleanor was immortalized by the Somerset writer Thomas Haynes Bayly in his narrative poem *The Mistletoe Bough.*

'I'm weary of dancing now,' she cried;
'Here tarry a moment, I'll hide, I'll hide!
And, Lovell, be sure thou'rt first to trace
The clue to my secret lurking place.'
Away she ran, and her friends began
Each bower to search and each nook to scan;
And young Lovell cried, 'Oh! where dost thou hide?
I'm lonesome without thee, my own dear bride!' . . . .

Oh! sad was her fate - in sportive jest,
She hid from her lord in the old oak chest;
It closed with a spring and dreadful doom!
The bride lay clasped in her living tomb!

Eleanor's story also became the subject of a play, *The Fatal Chest*, by Charles Somerset, first staged at the Garrick Theatre, Whitechapel, in 1834. For this production, Sir Henry Bishop, composer of *Home, Sweet Home*, set Bayly's poem to so fine a melody that *The Mistletoe Bough* grew into a Victorian evergreen.

Behind the altar in the church at Bawdrip where she had been married, a monument erected by her bridegroom tells sadly of 'Eleanor, daughter and heiress of the family honour and estates who died June 14th 1681. Her afflicted husband mourned her, snatched away well nigh on her wedding day by a sudden and untimely fate.'

'Here We Come A-Wassailing'

MANY delightful old customs linger in Somerset, providing entertainment for residents and visitors from January to December.

Early in the year, on 17th January, Old Twelfth Night, the ancient ceremony called Wassailing the Apple Trees is enacted to ensure a good crop of apples (and thus plenty of cider!) in the autumn.

Several inns keep up the custom, including the *Pike and Musket* at Walton, near Street, and the *Butcher's Arms* in Carhampton. The participants gather in a circle round the oldest tree in the orchard, while one member fires a shotgun into its gnarled branches to scare away any lurking evil spirits. A youngster climbs the tree and places a cake dipped in cider among the boughs. Jugs of cider are poured on its roots to encourage copious growth. The chosen tree is toasted by everyone with cider spiced with nutmeg and ginger, drunk from a three-handled wassail cup. When all throats have been properly lubricated, the traditional wassail song bursts forth with great gusto.

Old apple tree, old apple tree
We've come to wassail thee.

To bear and to bow apples enow,
Hats full, caps full,
Three bushel bags full
Barn floors full and a little heap under the stairs.

All the singers then repair to the inn for further refreshment (cider, of course) and dancing.

On Shrove Tuesday the centuries-old ritual of Egg Shackling, once believed to promote fertility, is enjoyed by children at Stoke St Gregory school, near Curry Rivel, and Shepton Beauchamp school, near Ilminster. Each child brings an egg to school with his or her name inscribed on it. The eggs are 'shackled' (shuffled together) in a sieve, and the egg which remains uncracked for longest is proclaimed the winner. A variation of this takes place at Triscombe, in the Quantocks, where the eggs are rolled down a grassy slope. Once again, the least damaged egg wins a prize for its owner.

A delightful time of the year for many Minehead folk is the Hobby Horse Festival, which begins on May Day Eve, and continues until 2nd May. The Hobby Horse is a weird, unforgettable sight. It is made of a wooden boat-shaped frame, about eight feet long, carried on the shoulders of a man whose masked head sticks up through a hole in the middle. The top of the frame is covered with hundreds of ribbons, and a large sheet of canvas, decorated with dozens of differently-coloured circles, reaches to the ground to hide the human operator from sight.

The origins of the Hobby Horse are lost in the mists of time. It may be part of an old fertility rite, rejoicing at the end of winter and greeting the spring; it may hark back to the days of frequent Viking raids on the Bristol Channel ports, when two Minehead sailors, seeing the marauders approach, upended their boat and disguised

80

it as a dragon, (wearing it on their shoulders much as it is today), which frightened them off.

Nowadays, the Hobby Horse provides a most colourful spectacle as it parades through the town, accompanied by music on accordion and drum, and attended by masked men known as 'Gullivers', who joke with the crowds and persuade them to part with their money, which the Horse collects via a slit in the canvas. In the old days, anyone refusing to pay up was 'booted' painfully in the appropriate part of his anatomy. He was also likely to be struck forcefully with the heavy, swinging tail of the Horse. Any 'booting' that goes on now is purely for entertainment.

Compared with the boisterous fun and games of the Hobby Horse, sheep-shearing was a time of back-breaking exertion, which took place on the sheep farms in the hilly parts of the county immediately after Mid-summer Day. Farms in a particular area pooled their workforces so that each flock was dealt with in turn by the shearers, usually in a single day. They would then move on in a body to the next farm.

You might imagine that the hectic pace at which everyone laboured during the daylight hours would have left them exhausted by evening. Not so! The successful completion of the work was marked by nightly junketing. Huge amounts of food and drink were provided by each farm and consumed with alacrity by the shearers. In the middle of the table there was always a large bowl of furmity - wheat boiled with milk, sugar, figs and cinnamon. After hearty eating, men and women danced and sang until the early hours. What energy they had! Sadly, sheep-shearing festivals have almost died out, with the advent of quicker methods of shearing, but the largesse enjoyed by the workparty is recalled in this traditional song.

81

Wife, make us a dinner, spare flesh neither corne,
Make wafers and cake, for our sheep must be shorne;
At sheepe shearing, neighbours none other things crave
But good cheers and welcome like neighbours to have.

In the same way that the satisfactory end to shearing was
marked by a festival, so too was the bringing in of the
harvest. The village of East Brent, at the foot of the
450 ft tor of Brent Knoll, still celebrates this event on the
third Thursday in August with a Harvest Home, a day-
long affair involving everybody. The Venerable George
Denison, Archdeacon of Taunton, who was rector at East
Brent for 51 years, until his death in 1896 at the age of 91,
revived the Harvest Home festivities in 1857.

Harvest Home begins in the morning with the band
leading a procession of villagers who carry, among other
things, plum puddings, huge cheeses and loaves. This is
followed by a service of Thanksgiving at St Michael's
church. Appetites whetted by marching and singing, the
participants then make their way to an enormous mar-
quee erected for the occasion, decorated with ropes of
ivy, corn and flowers, where all relish the delicious food
prepared by the womenfolk. In the afternoon there are
races, a fancy-dress parade and a tug-of-war (so the men
can impress the ladies). The day ends with music and
dancing.

The last Thursday in October is a very special date in
Hinton St George, near Crewkerne, where the inhabitants celebrate Punkie Night. This custom stretches back
about 200 years, to a time when the villagers enjoyed
going to the St Luke's Day Fair at Chiselborough, three
miles away. On this particular occasion, the women and
children left the fair before darkness fell and made their
way home across the fields, leaving the menfolk behind

to drink and gossip. It seems that too much of both was done; night closed in with no sign of their return.

The exasperated women decided they would have to fetch the sozzled ones home, but had no lanterns to light the way across pitch-dark, muddy pastures. They cleverly improvised lights by digging up mangolds, scooping out the flesh, and inserting a candle whose flame shone eerily through holes in the skin. It is to be hoped that the unexpected sight of the weirdly flickering lanterns appearing out of nowhere gave the unsteady returning revellers a good fright.

The children of the village recall the event by parading down the wide main street carrying their own mangold lanterns, each carved with an elaborate design or grotesque features. At the head of the procession are the Punkie Night King and Queen, enthroned on a flower-decked float. As the children march along, they chant variations of the Punkie Night song.

Gie us a candle, gie us a light,
It's Punkie Night tonight,
It's Punkie Night tonight,
Adam and Eve wouldn't believe,
It's Punkie Night tonight.

As the year draws to a close, one last ancient ritual is kept. This is the burning of the Ashen Faggot, a West Country version of the Yule Log. The date varies slightly from place to place, but is usually Christmas Eve or Old Christmas Eve (5th January).

At Curry Rivel, on the edge of Sedgemoor, the ceremony has taken place for the last two centuries at what is now the *King William IV* public house. The Ashen Faggot is made of a bundle of ash logs securely tied together with brambles or withies. It is laid with great reverence in the fireplace by two of the oldest members of the party and ignited. As the Faggot burns, the withy bonds (usually six) burst open one by one. This is greeted by a great deal of cheering and drinking of toasts. It is traditional to make a secret wish each time this happens.

Other places in Somerset, such as *The Luttrell Arms* in Dunster, also burn an Ashen Faggot. It is believed to commemorate the time when the Shepherds burnt one to warm the Infant Jesus.

The Ashen Faggot, like the Yule Log, was kept alight throughout the twelve days of Christmas. As it died, the Wassailers were already on their way to the orchards to toast the apple trees.

Old apple tree, old apple tree,
We've come to wassail thee.

Sarah Biffin,
'The Astonishing
Curiousity'

D URING the 18th century, the West Country, with its wonderfully varied scenery, became a favourite haunt of painters, the most famous of whom, Thomas Gainsborough, arrived from Suffolk in 1759 aged 32, and remained for 15 years. In the 1760s he went on sketching trips in Somerset, staying with his friend Goodenough Earle at Barton Grange, four miles south of Taunton. The expressive portrait of *The Pitminster Boy* has immortalized the local lad who happily carried the great man's paints and brushes on these excursions.

In stark contrast to such celebrated artists is the tiny, deformed, 37 inch high figure of Somerset's own Sarah Biffin. She came from East Quantoxhead, a tranquil village on the seaward edge of the Quantocks near Bridgwater Bay, complete with 14th century stone church, thatched cottages, duck pond, and imposing Court House, a home of the Luttrell family for over 700 years.

Sarah was born in the village on 25th October 1784, the third child of Henry and Sarah Biffin. To their horror, the baby girl, although healthy, had no arms and only rudimentary legs. She was baptized six days later at St John's church, the register stating baldly that she was 'born without arms or legs'. In her childhood Sarah's parents tirelessly cared for their handicapped daughter, doing their best in lowly circumstances to make her as self-reliant as possible. Her naturally cheerful disposition coupled with a gritty determination to do things for herself endeared her to her family. To their amazement she learnt to sew using her mouth, becoming exceptionally adroit at making her own clothes, managing needle, thread and scissors very skilfully. She also started to paint, demonstrating startling artistic ability. She held the brush by gripping the end with her lips and tongue and using her right shoulder stump to control the movement of the brush.

In the late 1790s she was spotted by Emmanuel Dukes, an artist touring Somerset. He offered to look after her and give her tuition if she would travel around the country with him and his wife, exhibiting her skills at circuses and fairs. Sarah's parents were delighted for their daughter to have the chance of a better life, so she became a member of the Dukes family. It seems she was cared for very kindly by them - indeed she remained with them for about 16 years - but received a paltry annual salary of £5.

In October 1812, she was at Swaffham Fair during the Race Week. According to a surviving handbill advertising her as 'the astonishing Curiousity', she sat 'in a Commodious Booth' where the spectators paid sixpence or a shilling to watch her sewing, writing and painting. Poor little Sarah had become a sideshow freak, gawped at and examined by curious and insensitive crowds. For every miniature painted on ivory that she completed for a customer, Mr Dukes charged three guineas. His confi-

86

dence in her was such that he promised to forfeit 1,000 guineas if she failed in her task.

A new chapter in her life began when she came to the notice of George, Earl of Morton, who was then Chamberlain of the Household to George III's consort, Queen Charlotte. The Earl asked the little artist to paint his portrait, but, to ensure no fraud was involved, took the picture away with him after each sitting. The finished portrait so impressed him that he showed it to the King, whose immediate interest in the artist encouraged the Earl to introduce her into Society. He arranged for her to have lessons from William Craig, Painter in Watercolours to the Queen and Miniature Painter to the Duke and Duchess of York. Sarah's extraordinary talents, combined with her chirpy nature, soon made her a favourite of the *haut monde*, enjoying the patronage of the Queen and other members of the Royal Family. Some of the pictures that she painted for her exalted clientele are inscribed 'Painted by Miss Biffin, without hands'. They vary in size tremendously - from a portrait 36 inches by 30 inches to miniatures of $2\frac{1}{2}$ inches - all executed most delicately. In 1821, she was awarded a silver medal by the Society of Artists.

Romance flared briefly in Sarah's life as she reached 40, with a short, disastrous marriage to a banker's clerk named Wright. Sadly, he was all wrong for her and they parted almost immediately. Rumours soon circulated that he had appropriated her money and then deserted her, but Sarah stoutly denied that he had touched her earnings.

In middle age, as her frightful disabilities began to take their toll, she found it increasingly difficult to work. Her great friend and benefactor, the Earl of Morton, died in 1827, much to her distress, and, after a while, her

Society friends forgot about her.

She retired to Liverpool in 1843, living very frugally on diminishing resources. She had been granted a pension of £12 a year by William IV, but was forced to use it as security for a loan. Providentially, her woeful plight came to the notice of one of her former patrons, the philanthropist Richard Rathbone, who set about fundraising. He wrote to hundreds of people who had bought her work, appealing for money. He hoped to raise £1,000, but managed just £300. One who did respond to his letter was Jenny Lind, the 'Swedish Nightingale'. She gave two concerts in Liverpool on 6th September and 8th September 1847, so it is just possible that the tiny artist was introduced to her. A number of Somerset people contributed, including John Poole, rector of the Quantock village of Enmore. (This was the man who, in 1810, built one of the first free primary schools in England).

The small income generated from the fund allowed Sarah to live a little more comfortably and retain her hard-won independence, but her courageous struggle ended three years later with her death on 2nd October 1850, aged 66. She was buried in St James' cemetery near Liverpool Cathedral, but her tombstone has long since disappeared.

In Liverpool City Museum is a watercolour self-portrait, presented by Richard Rathbone. It depicts a bonny woman in middle age, with her lack of arms cleverly concealed by a shawl. Although hardly anyone knows the name of Sarah Biffin nowadays, in her time she was sufficiently notable for Charles Dickens to mention her in two of his novels, *Nicholas Nickleby* (1838) and *Martin Chuzzlewit* (1843).

King Arthur's Cross

HIC JACET SEPULTUS INCLITUS REX ARTURIUS IN INSULA AVALONIA

'Here lies buried the renowned King Arthur in the Isle of Avalon'

T HESE words, crudely carved on a leaden cross, seemed to solve one of the great mysteries of Dark Age Britain - the whereabouts of the grave of Arthur, sixth century High King, Christian hero and legendary warrior.

The cross was discovered in 1190 at Glastonbury, an island of limestone and sandstone rising 500 ft above marshlands which were once connected by tidal channels to the sea. The Benedictine monks of the Abbey came across it while excavating a site in their own cemetery, prompted by no less a personage than the King of England, Henry II. He had been told by a Welsh 'singer of the past' that Arthur was lying in the Abbey graveyard between two pyramids. Since the continuing prophecies of Arthur's return unsettled the Plantagenet monarch, he was undoubtedly keen to find a body which might be Arthur's, so putting paid to the hopes of those who believed he would come back to reclaim his

kingdom. A certain amount of regal pressure was put on the monks to start digging.

However, the monks were already fully occupied with an extensive programme of rebuilding necessitated by a disastrous fire in May 1184, which had destroyed not only the Norman Abbey but the ancient, greatly venerated Old Church - **Vetusta Ecclesia** - as well. Henry contributed generously, thus applying a little more pressure, but time ran out for him - he was in his own burial place at Fontevrault, France, a year before the excavations at Glastonbury produced the proof he had so desired.

It has been suggested that the monks were spurred into action by a need for money. Henry's son Richard (the Lionheart), who spent just ten months of his ten year reign in England, was only interested in extorting cash from his subjects for the Third Crusade, and had no intention of handing any over to the Abbey. A new object of veneration was, it is said, necessary to replace the Old Church and its sacred relics which would attract pilgrims.

The two 'pyramids' mentioned to Henry by the Welsh bard were easy enough to locate; they were the weathered remains of stone Saxon memorial crosses, standing near the boundary of the monks' cemetery, about 40 ft south of the Old Church site. Rising up some 26 ft and 18 ft respectively, the tapering shafts could be described as 'pyramids'. So the monks set to work, digging a large hole between the crosses. They had reached a depth of seven ft when their spades clanged against something solid. Hurriedly clearing away the earth, they uncovered a massive stone slab. Heaving it to one side, they first set eyes on the leaden cross which commemorated Arthur.

By now, they were convinced that a few feet further down they would find the High King's tomb. With mounting anticipation and increasing difficulty the excavation continued unabated. At last, at a depth of 16 ft, they unearthed a coffin made from a hollowed-out oak trunk. Inside were the skeletons of two people, one much bigger than the other.

Careful examination of the bones revealed the large skeleton to be that of an extremely tall man, whose skull clearly showed the dreadful damage inflicted by a death-dealing blow. The other bones belonged to a small woman - a tress of golden hair crumbled to dust when one of the brothers tried to pick it up. Had they found Arthur and Guinevere? The Abbot believed they had. A new object of veneration had been provided. The bones were reverentially placed in separate caskets, painted with the portraits of Arthur and his Queen, and stored in the Abbey treasury.

At Easter, 1278, another King of England came with his Queen to Glastonbury. This was Edward I, accompanied by Eleanor of Castille, making a royal visit to view Arthur's bones. Legends of Arthur and his Knights of the Round Table were immensely popular throughout England and Wales in the Middle Ages, fuelled by Geoffrey of Monmouth's highly fanciful account of the High King's life published in the *History of the Kings of Britain* (1136). Edward was naturally interested in the story of the hidden grave, but probably had an ulterior motive; an astute political thinker, he knew that if the rebellious Welsh could be convinced that Arthur was dead, and not waiting for the right moment to overthrow the 'foreign' king, they would lose heart.

Once Edward had seen the bones, they were wrapped in precious silks, returned to their separate caskets, and placed in a specially-constructed black marble tomb in front of the High Altar in the new Abbey church.

During the next three centuries, the Abbey at Glastonbury grew steadily richer and more powerful. Extensive manorial holdings were acquired, and as the Benedictines prospered, so they enlarged the church, which was eventually an incredible 550 ft long. Then, in 1536, the Dissolution of the Monasteries began. Glastonbury, because of its unique history and extreme sanctity, was one of the last to fall, but Henry VIII's Commissioners finally closed in. They arrived on 22nd September 1539, and searched diligently for any sign of offence against the despotic Tudor monarch. A book was discovered in the library which disagreed with Henry's divorce from Catherine of Aragon. The 80 year old Abbot, Richard Whiting, was ordered to take the Oath of Supremacy, but obstinately refused. He was immediately arrested, sent to the Tower of London, and, two months later, taken to Wells for a sham trial. He was, of course, convicted of treason. The 61st and last Abbot of Glastonbury was hanged, with two of his monks, high up on Tor Hill, so that all the occupants of town and Abbey could witness his shameful death. His body was dismembered, the pieces being exhibited in Bath, Bridgwater, Ilchester and Wells as a ghastly reminder to the King's opponents. As a final insult, his head was stuck on the Abbey gate.

The glorious days of Glastonbury Abbey were over. Its buildings were vandalized, stripped of anything that could be carted away, and gradually dismantled, as local people began to use the beautiful stone for their own dwellings. Nowadays, the ruins give little idea of the magnificence of the Abbey that was once the greatest in the land.

What happened to the marble tomb? It, too, was broken up and the sacred relics dispersed. The leaden cross *was* preserved; the historian William Camden published a drawing of it in the sixth edition of his *Britannia* (1607); in the 18th century it was known to be in Wells, but has since vanished.

Even though the bones have probably long ago crumbled to dust and the original grave been filled and covered over, the puzzle remains. Was it Arthur? Although conclusive proof would be impossible to provide, it is at least possible to challenge the sceptics who believe that the grave-finding episode in 1190 was nothing more than a tremendous publicity stunt, a gigantic fraud, designed both to please the King and encourage pilgrims to visit the Abbey and part with their cash. The fact remains that the monks never had to use the tomb to attract visitors to such an ancient, holy place - they came anyway, thousands of them, from kings to peasants. No other site has claimed to be the Isle of Avalon, and nobody else has uncovered a grave purporting to be Arthur's, or produced a memorial cross. The lettering on the cross is believed to have been 10th century, not 12th century, as one might expect.

For the monks to have found the cross at a depth of seven feet is significant. When St Dunstan was made Abbot of Glastonbury in AD 943, he began a grand reconstruction of the monastic buildings. The graveyard, already full to overflowing, could hold no more bodies. He solved the problem by erecting a retaining wall around the cemetery and filling it with earth, effectively creating a second layer. This would account for both the position of the cross marking Arthur's grave, and for its 10th century style of lettering. Extensive excavations, carried out in 1962 by the archaeologist and historian C.A. Ralegh Radford confirmed that the monks had dug exactly where they claimed, since he was able accurately to date the stone chippings used in filling the hole.

Glastonbury is not the only place in Somerset with a strong Arthurian tradition. For centuries, many people believed that the 500ft high hill fort at South Cadbury was the 'hollow hill' in which Arthur and his knights lay sleeping. The steep sides of the hill had been heavily fortified with a number of ramparts long before the Romans invaded Britain. During the Occupation, the fort was overrun and partially wrecked. But at the beginning of the 6th century it was reoccupied, and refortified along its entire 1,200 yard perimeter. As an army base, it was ideally situated for campaigns against the Saxon marauders. It had to have been inhabited by a large, well-organized force under a powerful military leader - it was just too big for a petty princeling. We might assume that this was Arthur's headquarters and Cadbury Castle was Camelot. From his lofty viewpoint the King could see, eleven miles north-west across the marshy ground, the Tor at Glastonbury. If he chose for himself his last resting place, what could have been more fitting for a Christian leader than the holiest ground in England - beside the Old Church at Glastonbury?

The Parson,
the Turk and
the Whistling Ghost

A T THE foot of Dunkery Beacon, 'the haighest place
on Hexmoor', as John Fry says in *Lorna Doone*,
nestles the beautiful, secluded village of Luccombe. This
was the home of Dr Henry Byam, the celebrated fighting
Cavalier parson whose life was peppered with excitement and eventfulness.

He was born in Luccombe on 31st August 1580, the
eldest son of the local rector. Educated at Exeter College, Oxford, he succeeded his father as the rector of
Luccombe in 1612. Two years later, he also acquired,
from his father in law, the living at nearby Selworthy.
Before long, he won the reputation for being 'the most
acute and eminent preacher of his age', and his fame
spread far beyond the boundaries of Exmoor.

When the Civil War began in 1642, the Byam family
were the first in the district to take up arms for King
Charles I. Four of Henry's sons became captains in the
troop that he helped to raise for the Royalists. In March
1645, he was forced to flee from Luccombe and, accom-
panying young Prince Charles, escaped to the Scilly Isles.

Six weeks later, in the nick of time, he sailed with the royal fugitive to Jersey, where he acted as his chaplain, remaining until 1651. On returning to Somerset, he discovered that his estates had been confiscated by Cromwell.

During the Commonwealth he lived in comparative obscurity, largely confined to Exmoor, but, with the Restoration of King Charles II, his loyalty was at last rewarded; he was appointed Canon of Exeter and Prebendary of Wells. He died on 16th June 1669 at the age of 89 and was buried in the chancel of St Mary's, Luccombe. An elaborately carved altar-tomb, chronicling his many achievements, occupies the place of honour in the church. But what you will not find recounted on the tomb are two decidedly odd episodes in his distinguished life.

The first involved an unfortunate young man who 'turned Turk' after being captured by pirates and enslaved in Algiers. In the mid 1620s, when this happened, there were an estimated 1,500 English prisoners, mostly from Somerset, Devon and Cornwall, being held at Turkish bases in North Africa. The Turks went to enormous lengths to obtain slaves; they regularly attacked West Country villages, hauling men out of cottages and hostelries and bearing them swiftly away into the English Channel. This particular Somerset lad was perhaps captured during a raid along the coast north of Minehead.

His life as a slave must have been appalling, since he almost inevitably worked in the galleys, stripped naked in the hot and stinking conditions below decks. He would have pulled a 15 foot oar for sometimes ten hours without rest. He would have been chained to a plank and frequently lashed. His food consisted of a few biscuits or gruel; his drink, vinegar and water with some drops of oil. If he had collapsed, he would have been tossed overboard. Loss of life was of no consequence to the Turks, who sometimes valued a slave at the cost of an onion.

In 1624, the English Parliament proposed launching an appeal to buy the release of the captives, but King James did nothing except to issue Letters Patent for the purpose. The best way for a captive to survive was to renounce Christianity and 'turn Turk'. The Turks, who attached great significance to this, immediately made conditions easier for a convert. Our young fellow chose this course and, taking advantage of his improved situation, chanced all and escaped, eventually finding his way back to Minehead in March 1627.

One might imagine that, apart from general rejoicing, this was the end of his tale. Far from it - he was now a Mohammedan and Infidel. And so a special service was held at the parish church of St Michael's in Minehead on 16th March for the 're-admission of a Relapsed into our Church.' The occasion was sufficiently important for the famous Dr Byam to be prevailed upon to journey in from Luccombe to conduct a unique ceremony. The 'young Turk' had to stand before the congregation in his Muslim clothes, while the good Doctor declaimed an appropriately momentous oration. Here is one of the high points, as he addressed the sinner:

'Give glory to God, sing praises to Him who hath delivered your soul from the nethermost hell. When I think upon your Turkish attire, I do remember Adam and his fig-leaf breeches; they could neither conceal his shame, nor cover his nakedness . . . .
How could you hope, in this unsanctified habit, to attain Heaven?'

By the end of the service, the lad, having cast off his wanton faith and garments, was restored to the Church and, we must believe, lived happily ever after.

Seven years later, Dr Byam was again drawn into Minehead affairs, this time by the advent of the Whistling Ghost. He began to hear stories about the unearthly carryings-on of a recently deceased widow, Susan Leakey, who had been buried at St Michael's on 5th November 1634. Minehead folk, ignoring their local clergyman, Mr Heathfield (a man devoted more to the bottle than to his parishioners), came over to Luccombe with increasingly desperate reports.

Dr Byam learnt that Mrs Leakey, whose only son Alexander was a prosperous shipowner, had been a delightful person, well liked by her friends and neighbours for her amiable disposition. But now she had returned as a ghost, and her phantom was altogether different. It terrified people with its irascible behaviour and frightening demeanour. It was no spectral slouch, either, for it haunted by night and day, in the streets, in homes, in the fields, along the shore and even at sea. The lady was easily recognizable since she always wore the same clothes, 'a black gown, a white stomacher of shagge, and a kercher on her head.'

We do not know what Dr Byam made of these initial reports, but he certainly must have blinked when he heard about Mrs Leakey's meeting with the local doctor. The man had been out walking when the ghost suddenly appeared in front of him, standing by a stile. As he approached her, she indicated her wish to be helped over, which he did, rather gingerly. Off she sped to the next stile, reaching it well before him, perching on top and then refusing to budge. Only with the utmost difficulty was he able to manoeuvre round her. Alighting on the other side, he began to stride out, when he received a mighty kick in the pants to help him on his way.

Finally, word reached Luccombe that Mrs Leakey was now sinking ships. She would appear on the decks of boats leaving the harbour, and, blowing loudly on a whistle, raise such a storm that the mountainous waves engulfed the vessels and sent them to the bottom. Dr Byam was informed that she had started on her own son's ships, destroying the valuable business he had established, and bringing him to the verge of ruin. With many people now on the brink of hysteria, the parson decided to take action, and asked the Bishop of Bath and Wells to authorize a formal investigation.

The Bishop set up a Commission of Inquiry on which he himself served with Sir Robert Phelipps of Montacute and the Rector of Kingweston. They sifted all the evidence and carried out a number of interviews, but rejected most of the testimony as unreliable. The Rev Heathfield's deposition, for example, was discounted because of his drunkenness. In the end, the Commission dismissed the whole idea of the ghost: 'we are yet of opinion and doe beleive that there never was any such apparition at all, but that it is an imposture, devise, and fraud for some particular ends, but what they are wee know not.' This judgement, later endorsed by Archbishop Laud, can be inspected in the *Calendar of State Papers, Domestic Series, 1637-8.*

After the findings of the commission had been made known, the Whistling Ghost was never seen in Minehead again. Whatever the truth of the affair, the good sense of Henry Byam seems to have had a beneficial effect and laid Mrs Leakey finally to rest.

A
Dying Flame

A N auctioneer, a clergyman and a bewigged barrister
met one summer evening at an inn to maintain a tradition that has endured for 500 years. The date was Tuesday 19th July 1988; the place was the Manor Inn, Manor
Road, in the Sedgemoor village of Chedzoy; the ceremony was the candle auction, held every 21 years since
1490.

The auction was not, as one might imagine, an opportunity to corner the market in candles but to acquire the
lease for the next 21 years of a piece of land called
Church Acre. The excitement of the occasion was due to
the unconventional method of conducting the sale. A
half-inch stump of tallow candle was lit and placed in
front of the auctioneer, who invited offers for the field.
Since the successful bid would be the last one before the
candle flame died, the initial amounts suggested were
rather paltry, beginning at just £2. After 20 minutes, the
price had climbed to £1,400 while the candle had sunk
almost to extinction. Fast and furious bidding in the last
few moments produced a final bid of £1,650 from Mr
Howes of Bridgwater, and plenty of fun for the 100 or so
spectators.

Although candle auctions were not uncommon in the 17th century, taking place in London as a means of selling goods imported from the Orient, the Chedzoy auction is probably the oldest known. Church Acre, situated on the Bridgwater side of the village, is believed to have been bequeathed to the church by Sir Richard Sydenham, who intended the land to be an arable plot. Nowadays it may be put to any agricultural use, but no permanent buildings are allowed to be erected.

The money raised at the auction goes to the church building fund. The price of the lease rose over the years, from £4 in 1694 to £68 in 1904; 1946 saw a record bid of £125, partly caused by the unusual length of time that the candle kept burning - an amazing 41 minutes! By 1967, interest in the old custom was so great that the upstairs room at the Manor Inn usually reserved for the event had to be abandoned in favour of an outdoor auction to make room for the 300 lookers-on. An eminent clergyman present on that day was Edward Henderson, Bishop of Bath and Wells, who inadvertently blew out the candle!

The last holder of Church Acre kept ducks, geese and chickens on the plot. The new occupant, who took over at Michaelmas, has put horses on it. Whoever leases the land must keep it free of weeds and use it 'according to the methods and practices of local husbandry'. The next auction will take place in 2009 - rather a long time to wait if you want to see this quaint custom enacted again.

Chedzoy itself is of great historical significance even without the bonus of a candle auction. Its name is derived from 'Cedda', a Saxon personal name, and 'ey' meaning isle - hence Cedda's isle. Together with Weston-zoyland and Middlezoy, it occupies the Sowy Island, 2,000 acres of silt on the edge of Sedgemoor - the place where so many Somerset men died in July 1685, in the last pitched battle to be fought on English soil.

If you walk around the outside of St Mary's church you will notice on the walls some strange marks thought at one time to have been caused by the men of Chedzoy honing their scythes before marching off to fight for the rebel Duke of Monmouth. In reality, they were made a century earlier by men sharpening their arrows before archery practice in the churchyard on Sundays after Divine Service. And in reality, too, none of the 300 inhabitants left the village to join the Duke. Chedzoy remained loyal to King James II, largely through the persuasive powers of its long-serving rector, Andrew Paschall, an ardent Royalist. Nevertheless, there were Monmouth sympathizers.

One of these, William Sparke, a farmer, spotted the advance of a large body of Royalist troops - led by the Earl of Feversham. He rushed to the top of St Mary's tower and watched through his spyglass as they made camp at Westonzoyland. Summoning his herdsman, Benjamin Godfrey, he sent him posthaste to the Duke's headquarters with the information. Godfrey reported to Monmouth and received a guinea for his pains. Knowing the marshy areas of Sedgemoor like the back of his hand, he offered to guide the insurgents safely across in the dead of night so that a surprise attack could be launched at the unsuspecting Royalists. Monmouth, desperate for a victory to inspire his dwindling army, agreed to the plan.

Unluckily for him, the night became so foggy that even the experienced Godfrey lost his bearings and missed the vital crossing point over the waterfilled Langmoor Rhine, causing chaotic disarray at the very moment when speed and silence were crucial. Also unluckily, the King's men were not as sozzled on the local cider as had been hoped. A wakeful sentry gave the alarm, and within minutes six Royal battalions were ready for action.

The resulting slaughter which took place, as Monmouth's untrained army came to grips with disciplined soldiers and were massacred in their hundreds, is grimly recorded on the memorial stone erected in the Gravefield, Langmoor Drove, Sedgemoor.

TO THE GLORY OF GOD
AND IN MEMORY OF ALL THOSE WHO
DOING THE RIGHT AS THEY GAVE IT
FELL IN THE BATTLE OF SEDGEMOOR
6TH JULY 1685
AND LIE BURIED IN THIS FIELD
OR WHO FOR THEIR SHARE IN THE FIGHT
SUFFERED DEATH
PUNISHMENT OR TRANSPORTATION

Chedzoy was directly involved in the ghastly aftermath of the battle: of the 500 captured rebels incarcerated in Westonzoyland church the following day, 22 were summarily executed nearby. The cost of the hangings and burials, £12 4s 1d, was charged to the parish.

The Rev Andrew Paschall, who had quietly gone with his family to Honiton at the first sign of trouble, returned the day after the bloodbath. He immediately began writing an account of the action, now widely regarded as a most valuable contemporary report. He also drew an accurate sketch map of the battlefield, containing information from eye witnesses. These two important documents were discovered in 1939 at Hoare's Bank in the City of London, but you can see copies in Westonzoyland church. Paschall would be astonished to know that his narrative has been read by so many thousands of people, including the man who refers to it in his book *Marlborough: his Life and Times*, Sir Winston Churchill.

104

The
Rotten Branches

YOUNG female servants have always been easy prey for bestial masters to beat and abuse, and there are many heart-rending tales of girls turned out to starve when they no longer pleased their employers. Jane Buttersworth's story is a little different - she was viciously battered to death in 1740 by two women - her mistress Elizabeth Branch and Mrs Branch's daughter, Betty. The discovery of the murder at Highchurch Farm, in the parish of Hemington, near Frome, and the subsequent trial and execution of the culprits at Ilchester, caused a sensation.

Elizabeth Branch was born Elizabeth Parry in Bristol, the daughter of well-to-do parents who gave her a decent education and upbringing. But she was such a belligerent, bad tempered child that her anxious mother warned her of the difficulty of finding a suitable husband. However, Elizabeth managed to curb her violent inclinations long enough to ensnare, with the help of a sizeable dowry, an unsuspecting attorney named Benjamin Branch. She bore him two children, Betty and a son, Parry. The marriage was a disaster. The mild mannered, kindly lawyer was horrified to learn of the brutality with

which his wife treated the servants, and protested at her behaviour. Her reputation became such that it was a real problem to get any but the poorest sort of girl to work in the house. Little Betty grew up exhibiting the same desire to inflict pain on others, but Parry seems to have been as inoffensive as his father. The unhappy Mr Branch soon gave up the ghost, amid suggestions that he had been poisoned.

The Widow Branch, with a comfortable income to maintain her, was now absolutely free to cut loose on her maidservants. Like most bullies, she was also a coward, wary of attacking the adult males in her house, although there was an incident involving a young lad, Henry Butler, who was stripped and lewdly humiliated.

In September, 1739, two new maidservants joined the sour, unwelcoming Branch family at Highchurch Farm. They were Ann James and Jane Buttersworth. Ann was a robust Welsh lass, well able to take care of herself, but Jane was quite a different sort of girl. A woebegone homeless waif, she mistakenly believed she had been apprenticed to Mrs Branch, and therefore considered herself a virtual prisoner, unable to escape from the persecution she very quickly began to suffer. During the next few months, she was frequently chastised for the most trivial offences, even though she always behaved well and worked hard. Her very meekness made her a wonderful target for the Branch women. Ann sometimes tried to intervene, but was sharply told to mind her own business.

On Tuesday 12th February 1740, Jane was sent to Faulkland village, half a mile distant, to buy some bran from Anthony Budd. She returned empty handed, saying there was none to be had. At eight o'clock next morning, the Budd's son, William, arrived at the farm to help Parry cut and stack firewood. Naturally, Mrs Branch wanted to know why there had been no bran for sale. William told her they had plenty of bran but no customers. With her temper rising, Mrs Branch shouted for Jane to come and explain herself. Jane swore she was telling the truth, but her employer, always ready to believe the worst, sent Ann to Faulkland to ascertain what had happened.

By nine o'clock, Ann was at the Budd's house, where Margaret Budd insisted that Jane had not called. In fact what had happened was that Jane had been sent on her errand without any money, and Mrs Budd refused to allow her credit. The true facts behind the story did not emerge until it was too late for Jane.

When Ann returned home, Betty and Jane were feeding the calves. She noticed at once that Jane's elbow was bleeding. When Betty heard that Margaret Budd denied seeing Jane, she began to belabour her about the head, and then ordered the two girls into the kitchen. On entering, Ann saw some large sticks lying on the windowsill, which Mrs Branch and her daughter grabbed. Flinging Jane face down on the floor, Betty knelt on her neck while her mother whipped her until her clothes were bloodsoaked, deaf both to the maid's screams and Ann's horrified protests.

Betty stood up to aim a few vicious kicks at Jane, which gave her a chance to struggle free. She managed to reach the hall, but was caught again and dragged back to the kitchen with blood pouring down her face. Ordered to clean herself, she made a feeble attempt to wash off the blood, but was overcome with faintness. Seeming not the least perturbed by her savagery, Mrs Branch told the battered girl to dust and sweep the parlour. Jane crept, sobbing piteously, from the room.

When she thought it was safe to move, Ann went to look for her, and found her leaning on the broom, too giddy to stir. Thoroughly frightened, she rushed to tell Mrs Branch that Jane was badly hurt and needed help. The woman laughed cruelly, saying that she was just trying to avoid working, and if she did not get cracking she would get another dose. Ann half carried the girl into the fresh air, where the ghastly Betty was waiting with a bucket of water which she threw over them both. Ann cried that Jane could not possibly do any work, where-upon Mrs Branch shouted 'Do it, or I'll break your neck!'

Ann was dispatched on another errand, and returned to find Jane lying on the brewhouse floor, almost uncon-scious. She lifted her into a chair, but was immediately discovered by Betty, who told Jane that if she did not get on with the washing up she would rub her wounds with salt. The maid replied faintly 'I will, Miss', but made no attempt to move. Pushing her onto the floor, Betty fulfilled her threat and rubbed salt into all the cuts and abrasions on her body. The girl lay motionless, mutter-ing 'I will, miss'. Eventually, she was hauled into the kitchen by the Branches, where a clean cap was put on to disguise her head wounds.

At about six o'clock, Ann tried to rouse her, but failed. Realizing she was dead, she ran to tell Mrs Branch, who hotly denied it, and told Ann to put her in bed, where she could recover. Later, the Branch women forced Ann into bed with the body, where she lay sleepless all through the night, trying not to touch the stiffening corpse. In the morning, Mrs Branch had to admit that Jane was dead.

All that day, the body lay unattended, but on Friday William Budd was sent to Frome, four miles away, to buy a coffin and shroud. Poor Ann was made to help clean the corpse with Mrs Branch, who at last seemed alarmed by what she had done, and tried to conceal the dreadful injuries under the shroud. There was dried blood on Jane's arms, neck, face and legs. For yet another day the body lay in the room, but on Sunday morning it was put into the coffin by the Branches and a manservant, John Lawrence. Betty hid the bloodsoaked clothes in the apple cellar. In the evening, Jane was buried in Hemington churchyard. After the funeral, Mrs Branch aroused the suspicions of Francis Coombes, the sexton, by questioning him at length about the depth of the grave.

During the next few days, rumours of foul play gradually took hold in the village, so two local men, Robert Carver and John Marchant, decided to investigate. On the evening of Ash Wednesday, 20th February, they obtained the church key under a pretence of bellringing practice, dug up the coffin, and placed it in the church. They were surprised to see how securely the lid had been fastened down with huge nails. Having prised it open, they asked some of the village women to look carefully at the body. When the shroud was removed, all were sickened at the sight of the maltreated girl. Then she was gently covered again, the church doors securely locked, and the grisly findings reported to John Cradock, the churchwarden.

Next morning, the constable from Faulkland, together with Cradock, Carver and Marchant, arrested the Branches, Ann James and John Lawrence on suspicion of murder. Jane's body was examined by a surgeon, Dr Salmon. She had suffered a huge blood loss, and he thought her injuries severe enough to have killed an ox. An intensive search of the house revealed the bloody sticks, but not the clothes hidden in the apple cellar.

The Branch women and the two servants were held in custody at the Faulkland Inn, where Ann volunteered to make a statement. The Coroner's inquest, on 22nd and 23rd February 1740, gave her the opportunity to relate the appalling chain of events leading up to the murder. Three days later, she repeated her statement, without any variations, to the Justice of the Peace, Joseph Houlton. William Budd also made a statement which tallied with hers.

On Monday, 31st March, Elizabeth and Betty Branch were tried for the murder of Jane Buttersworth before the Hon Mr Justice Chapple at the Somerset Assizes. Mrs Branch, a wealthy woman, retained eight defence lawyers in a frantic effort to avoid the inevitable. They sought to persuade the jury that the prosecution witnesses were all liars who had been attempting to use the natural death of the little servant to extort money from the Branches, by threatening to accuse them of murder. Since each of the eight attorneys made the same points over and over, insisting that Jane suffered from fits and had fallen downstairs, they were not in the least convincing. The Crown lawyer remarked contemptuously on their 'large and copious Reply' to the charge, before proceeding smoothly to the prosecution.

The trial lasted about six hours, including the judge's summing-up. The jury conferred briefly without leaving the courtroom and quickly brought in a verdict of 'Guilty'. Mrs Branch showed not the least sign of emotion, although her temper erupted as she kicked one of the women standing by the Bar who had given evidence against her. Sentence of death was passed on both women. Mrs Branch still seemed unconcerned, but Betty collapsed and was unconscious for three quarters of an hour. A woman warder tried to revive her with a drink, but Mrs Branch, at last showing some feeling, cried out 'Zounds, what are you going to do? Had not she better die thus than live to be hang'd?'

After being sentenced, the women were transferred to the damp and putrid Ilchester gaol, where Somerset's worst offenders were held awaiting execution. The date was set for 3rd May, allowing the older woman time to settle her affairs and petition for a reprieve. While in prison, Mrs Branch seemed interested only in the mechanics of hanging and how the noose was best positioned, but Betty began to show signs of contrition. Once or twice, a kindly gaoler let her out to walk with him to his house at Limington, about a mile away. She wanted to be buried in Limington churchyard, but the vicar forbade it.

By Friday 2nd May, the women had given up all hope of a reprieve. They asked for the execution to take place very early the following morning, before too many people could arrive to watch and jeer. The country folk were so enraged by the cruelty of the killing that thousands were expected to attend the hangings.

When the party from the prison came to the place of execution, they found that a section of the gallows had been destroyed. Mrs Branch was so anxious about the time that she asked to be hanged on a nearby tree. However, the gibbet was soon repaired and ready for use. Having learnt how a noose should be properly fitted, Mrs Branch put it round her daughter's neck herself. She decided to address the small number of spectators who were beginning to gather, expressing remorse for her brutality, but also trying to excuse herself.

'Keep your passions within due bounds; let them not get the mastery over you, lest they bring you to this ignoble end. I am fully punished for all my severities; and it is true I did strike my maid, but not with a design to kill her, and so far I think the sentence about to be executed upon me is unjust!'

She also regretted that her behaviour had affected Betty. 'I have, by my example, and by my commands, made my daughter guilty with me of the same follies, cruelties, and barbarities, and thereby have involved her in the same punishment with myself.'

After she had finished, Betty, quaking with fright, made her own plaintive speech.

'Good people, pity my unhappy case, who, while young, was trained up in the paths of cruelty and barbarity; and let all present take warning by my unhappy end, so as to avoid the like crimes. You see I am cut off in the prime of life, in the midst of my days. Good people, pray for me!'

The execution took place without further delay in broad daylight, at six o'clock. An hour later, the rotten Branches were cut down and removed to Ilchester churchyard for burial.

The Magic
of Wookey

Two miles from the bustling cathedral city of Wells, at the foot of the Mendips, is an enchanted hill; take a walk right into it and one of Somerset's most awe-inspiring sights will be revealed - the ancient series of caverns known as Wookey Hole.

The Mendip Hills are honeycombed with caves which began to be fashioned millions of years ago by drops of water slowly dissolving the carboniferous limestone which forms the core. Many of these remain unknown, unexplored, impenetrable; some gave shelter to mammoth, cave bear, woolly rhinoceros, wolf, bison, hyena and man. Wookey Hole proved a secure home for Stone Age and Iron Age families; the long narrow entrance was easily defended, the large cavern provided ample accommodation at a comfortable temperature - a steady 50 F - and the newly-born river Axe flowing through the cave supplied constant fresh water. (The river bursts out of the cliff-face at the rate of twelve million gallons a day a short way from the entrance.) Refugees from the Roman invaders found sanctuary here, and so, apparently, did an old crone known as the Witch of Wookey.

The Witch seems to have been a solitary inhabitant of

the cave, credited with evil powers by the local people, whose appearance was so repellent that Henry Harrington, describing her in 1756 wrote

'She blasted every plant around
And blister'd every flock.'

Her ghastly deeds were said to include supplementing her diet with lightly-boiled children cooked on the premises. In 1912, the celebrated explorer of Mendip caves, Herbert Balch, made some exciting discoveries about her in the cavern called the Great Cave. He found an iron milking pot, a toothed comb made from deer antler, a dagger, a polished crystalline ball carved from a stalagmite, and the greater part of a skeleton; he also unearthed cooked human bones . . . .

Whether the Witch was murdered or simply died of old age, nobody knows. Her remains and possessions are on display in Wells Museum. Legend accords her a more dramatic end; a monk from Glastonbury confronted the hag in her den, splashed her with holy water and turned her instantly to stone. And there she sits to this day, a weirdly-shaped stalagmite, imprisoned in her kitchen, gazing hopelessly at the river escaping easily to the outside world.

Wookey Hole and its unwilling occupant have attracted visitors for at least 500 years; the writer William of Worcester went there in 1470. By the time of Queen Anne, the locals had cottoned on to the idea of charging for admission: 6d (old money) a head, with candles and a mug of beer thrown in. By then, Wookey's fame was such that Alexander Pope asked for some stalactites to furnish his celebrated grotto at Twickenham. These were duly sent, and found their way into his *Verses on a*

Grotto by the River Thames:

'Where lingering Drops from Mineral Roofs distil,
And pointed Crystals break the sparkling Rill.'

One of the most vivid early prose descriptions came from
Celia Fiennes, journeying through the West Country at
the end of the 17th century.

'They phancy one of the rocks resembles a woman with
a great belly which the country people call the Witch
which made this cavity under ground for her enchant-
ments; the rocks are glistering and shine like diamonds,
and some you climbe over where one meets with the
congealed drops of water just like iceicles hanging down;
some of the stone is white like alabaster and glisters like
mettle; you walke for the most part in the large spaces
called the Roomes on a sandy floore the roofe so lofty
one can scarce discern the top and carry's a great eccho,
soe that takeing up a great stone . . . . and letting it fall
gives a report like a Cannon, which they . . . . call the
Shooteing the Cannons.'

Since Celia's visit, the many stalactites and stalagmites in
the caves that she admired, and the Witch herself, have
grown less than an inch. Her view of the subterranean
wonderland was necessarily restricted by the flickering
candles which were her source of light. She would have
been even more amazed if able to return in 1926, when
the installation of electric light unveiled all the hidden
beauty of the rocks and water; the pale limestone walls,
stained with manganese, iron oxide and lead, coloured
black, red, grey and yellow; the river, in dancing cascades
and quiet pools, changing from white to turquoise to

116

greenish-black. One result of the lighting was to encourage green ferns and mosses to grow in the cracks and fissures; cave bats and spiders, traditional companions of witches, unperturbed by the intrusion of humans into their world, live in the shadowy depths of the caverns.

Man's desire to penetrate deeper and deeper into the enchanted hill has led to many new chambers being discovered. Until 1935, only the first four caves had been explored; it was impossible to proceed further because the passage was underwater. But the invention of diving equipment made progress feasible. The very first attempt at cave diving in Britain using breathing apparatus was made here by Graham Balcombe and Penelope Powell in 1935. They reached as far as Chamber Seven. Thirteen years later, better equipment allowed divers to gain access to Chamber Nine, a vast cavern with a hundred ft high roof, and very deep water. Another 40 years has seen more and more caves investigated - the searchers have reached Chamber 25. Two divers have drowned during the expeditions - the second as recently as 1981 - but the challenge of Wookey Hole is irresistible to cave explorers.

Visitors to the caves can now walk for some 350 yards in the subterranean passages and specially constructed walkways, beginning with a descent on Hell's Ladder to the Witch's Kitchen and reaching as far as Chamber Nine with its spectacular stalactite formations before returning through a manmade tunnel to the outside world. It is an unforgettable experience.

Even so, there is more to see at Wookey Hole. Emerging from the caves, a short walk beside the river Axe brings you to the paper mill, where high quality handmade paper was first manufactured about 1610. It is still being made today, using the Victorian machinery installed by William Hodgkinson, a London stationer, who acquired the mill in 1848. He produced exquisitely watermarked paper for bank notes, and writing paper so luxurious that it was used by Queen Victoria. During the American Civil War, he also supplied paper for the Confederate bank notes isued at Richmond, Virginia. The Hodgkinson family owned the mill for a hundred years, bringing employment and prosperity to the area. They built homes, a church and a school; they even provided the instruments for the mill's brass band. At one time, 200 people worked here, many of whom were women whose job was to shred the cotton rags from which the paper was made. Around 1900, Wookey Hole Mill was producing 35,000 sheets of paper every week, and was Europe's largest rag-paper mill.

In 1973, the caves and mill were bought by Madame Tussaud's who made a number of improvements for the safety and enjoyment of visitors to the caves. The paper-making operation, sadly run down with the end of the Hodgkinson era, was triumphantly revived and new attractions such as the Old Penny Pier Arcade were introduced in the mill buildings.

The latest owners of Wookey Hole, eager to allow visitors some 'hands-on' fun, encourage them to have a go at making paper for themselves - a uniquely satisfying experience. Adjacent to the paper mill, the Cave and Cave Diving Museum reminds us all of the continuing fascination of Wookey Hole for dedicated explorers and for those looking for a little bit of magic. Wookey hole has it all.

The
Abode of Love

A GAPEMONITES. They sound as if they might be flowers or fossils. Actually, they were the followers of two self-proclaimed Messiahs whose scandalous behaviour deep in rural Somerset provoked banner headlines in newspapers throughout the country.

The first of these bizarre characters was Henry Prince, born in Bath in 1811. His early life was entirely unremarkable - he studied medicine at Guy's Hospital, qualified in 1832, and took up an appointment as Medical Officer in his home town. Ill health forced him to abandon his career within a few years, so he chose to become a theological student at St David's College, Lampeter, in 1837. He was eventually ordained as curate of Charlynch, near Bridgwater, where he was left in sole charge because the rector, Samuel Starkey, was ailing. He began to preach lengthy revivalist sermons, and was thrilled to discover the almost hypnotic power he exerted over his parishioners. Soon, his success led to extraordinary self-delusions. He became convinced he was the new Messiah, and toured the countryside proclaiming his divinity, with the newly-converted Reverend Starkey in tow.

By the sheer force of his magnetic personality he persuaded a number of people, mostly female, not only to follow him but also to contribute generously to his bank account, promising them a new and wonderful life as members of his Agapemonite community. He preferred the women to be young, pretty, and well-endowed both physically and financially. He had soon collected enough money to buy a mansion at Spaxton, not far from Charlynch, and, naming it the Agapemone or 'Abode of Love', moved in with his coterie.

The house, standing in five acres of well kept gardens, and enclosed by 15 ft high stone walls, was large and luxurious. Twenty bedrooms housed the women who were now completely under his spell. The very few male converts were not allowed to live in the house, but were confined to cottages in the grounds. Prince built a chapel adjoining the mansion where his adherents gathered to worship. But the chapel could hardly be described as a holy place - it was sumptuously furnished with blue velvet sofas and a blue Turkey carpet. In place of the altar was a billiard table, and there is no doubt that the 'Messiah' or 'Heavenly Bridegroom' (his secondary title, more apt than the first) encouraged his young ladies to shed their inhibitions, as well as their garments, upon its smooth surface. In short, the Agapemone was Prince's personal seraglio, bought and paid for by his enraptured handmaidens, who addressed him always as 'Beloved'.

The inhabitants of Spaxton, who might have been expected to complain to the authorities about the disorderly goings-on behind the high walls, were soothed by the generosity of the occupants, especially at Christmas.

The 'Beloved' made only occasional trips outside his mansion, but these excursions were quite magnificent events. He would ride into Bridgwater in a carriage

121

drawn by four matched bays, with outriders and heralds proclaiming 'Blessed is he who cometh in the name of the Lord'. The townspeople were impressed by the spectacle; the shopkeepers were delighted by the large amounts of cash deposited in their tills.

In 1860, a lawsuit brought in the Court of Chancery by a relative of one of the 'brides' who had yielded her entire fortune to Prince, inflicted some unwelcome publicity on the sect. The ecclesiastical authorities sprang into action and the 'Heavenly Bridegroom' was officially unfrocked. Unofficially, of course, he must have been in that state much of the time, until advancing years took their inevitable toll.

For half a century, the 'Beloved' ruled as an absolute monarch in his small kingdom. The ageing members of the sect lived in almost total seclusion, but were apparently content with their strange existence. However, the 'immortal' Henry Prince had a shock in store for them - he died suddenly on 8th March 1899 aged 88. He was quietly buried at night in the grounds of the Agapemone, his coffin interred upright ready for his expected 'Resurrection'.

His abrupt demise caused great perturbation among the Agapemonites. A new 'Bridegroom' would have to be found. The natural successor was another curate, who was at that time pastor of the London church established by Prince in the 1890s - the Ark of the Covenant at Clapton, near Hackney. His name was John Hugh Smyth-Pigott.

Born in 1852, he came from an old Somerset county family. His early career was more colourful than Prince's. He had been soldier, sailor, coffee planter and Salvationist before deciding to assume the mantle of the 'Beloved'. This man was a very different character from the deluded Henry Prince since he knew precisely what he was doing. He thought long and hard - for three years - before he took the plunge by announcing to his congregation that he was indeed the new 'Messiah' and would be moving to his residence at Spaxton forthwith.

His disclosures were leaked to the press, and thus came quickly to the ears of the general public, who, angry and indignant, gathered in large numbers outside his home at Clapton Common. He needed police protection until he managed to slip unobtrusively away from his house and into the welcoming arms of the Agapemonites of Spaxton.

A thorough weeding out process then took place. Most of the original members were now old and frail - not to his taste at all. A recruitment drive produced enough new converts to satisfy Smyth-Pigott's strict requirements - wealth, youth and a desire to please.

The new 'Heavenly Bridegroom' already had an earthly wife, Catherine, but also brought with him from London 'Sister' Ruth Preece, whom he introduced as his 'Chief Soul Bride'! She bore him two sons and a daughter, named Glory, Power and Hallelujah. The birth of these children provoked righteous indignation (with a touch of jealousy?) among local men, two of whom, in August 1908, attempted to tar and feather Smyth-Pigott, but were arrested and sent to prison for their pains.

However, the publicity caused by the assault jerked the Church of England into incredibly belated action once more. The following month, proceedings were instituted by the Rt Reverend George Wyndham Kennion, Bishop of Bath and Wells, under the Clergy Discipline Act. In the solemn surroundings of Wells Cathedral the Bishop pronounced a second unfrocking. Smyth-Pigott, manifestly unconcerned about the whole affair, just as

123

Prince had been, continued unabated his life of sensual luxury.

Around this time, an enterprising reporter, posing as a convert, was allowed into the Agapemone. He came out with an exclusive account of the inmates, of whom he counted 100, mostly women. He noted that the majority were good looking, rich, or both, and that reports of a decline in the community were completely false. Smyth-Pigott was at the height of his powers, although why he was so irresistible is impossible to explain, since he was tall and skinny with dark, thinning hair and spectacles. But he exuded an aura of sexual mastery that dominated the womenfolk of the Agapemone until his unlooked-for death in March 1927.

No other candidate presented himself to the bereaved ladies of Spaxton, neither did they appear to desire one. Newspapers published lurid articles headlined 'The Escapades of Sister Ruth', but, in truth, the surviving members of the sect lived out their lives in peaceful retirement. No more sexual gymnastics took place on the well-worn green baize of the billiard table; an era was over and Spaxton became respectable once more.

Stand
and Deliver!

A HIGHWAYMAN! In our mind's eye a vision is instantly conjured up of a romantic hero, cloaked and masked, brandishing a brace of pistols, astride a fiery coal-black steed. The reality, of course, was very different. The majority of 17th century highwaymen were dyed-in-the-wool villains, shabbily dressed and poorly mounted, eking out a precarious, and often surprisingly brief, existence robbing unprotected travellers. But one of the few whose looks and attire would not have disappointed us was a West Country lad called Tom Cox.

Born in 1666, the younger son of a gentleman, he grew into a startlingly handsome youth with a penchant for women and gambling, joint passions which soon swallowed up his rather meagre inheritance. Egged on by the shady characters with whom he spent his time, he decided the only cure for his unwonted penury was to take to the road and steal what he needed from those overburdened with guineas. He was moderately successful, but was arrested on three separate occasions and tried at the Assizes in Winchester, Gloucester and Worcester. Each time he was fortunate enough to be acquitted.

At his trial in Worcester, his attractiveness and elegant

garb (he liked to wear white waistcoat, breeches and stockings) caught the attention of a young gentlewoman. She promptly fell madly in love with him. Since she was not only pretty but had a fortune of £1500, Tom unhesitatingly agreed to marry her. However, far from settling down and becoming a good husband, he took less than two years to distribute her money around various gambling dens and brothels and to break her heart. Abandoning matrimony, he went back to his old trade. The highways and byways of Somerset began to receive his special attention.

On one occasion he was in Somerton, where he may well have stayed at the town's oldest hostelry - known simply as The Inn (now a private house called 'Cockspurs') - since it was ideally situated on the outskirts of the town. Leaving Somerton on the road to Castle Cary he encountered Thomas Killigrew, King Charles II's Jester, returning to his home in Cornwall. Mr Killigrew was commanded to 'Stand and deliver!', but made all manner of excuses for hanging on to his purse. He even asked Cox if he was playing a joke on him, whereupon the rogue smartly replied

'Nay, I am in earnest, for though you live by jesting, I can't; therefore deliver your money, before a brace of balls make the sun shine through your body.'

This unfriendly rejoinder persuaded the hapless courtier to part with his 25 guineas without more ado.

Another escapade involved a well-known brothel-keeper, Madame Box. Tom accosted her on the highway and demanded her money, but once again his intended victim put up spirited verbal resistance - so spirited that she and Tom began cursing virulently at one another, the old madam well able to hold her own. Also, as she had recognised her assailant as a recent customer at her establishment, she threatened to see him dangling on a gibbet. The highwayman had had enough; he bestowed a final tirade of stinging insults relating to her extreme ugliness and lack of teeth, ending

'Why do I stand spending by breath about such a toad as this, who's the common nuisance of a civilised neighbourhood! Come, come, you bitch, deliver your money, or else your life must be a sacrifice to my fury.'

He wrested the money from her grasp, while she continued to scream and shout abuse at him. Finally losing his temper, Tom vowed to teach her a lesson. He roughly stripped her of every article of clothing and galloped away, leaving her standing stark naked in the middle of the road - her frenzied shrieks ringing ever more faintly in his ears.

Now life took a grimmer turn; Cox was arrested after a hold-up near Chard and sent to the County Gaol at Ilchester. Towards the end of the 17th century this fetid prison, built beside the river Yeo, was bursting at the seams with felons and debtors awaiting trial and convicted criminals awaiting death. In fact, the over-crowding was so severe that less serious offenders were kept in an abandoned priory down the street. Cox would have been incarcerated in the cells reserved for male felons, situated next to the turnkey's lodge by the entrance gate. The convenience of this position was not lost on him as he racked his brains for a means of escape. Luckily, the gaoler was usually blind drunk by evening, so the nimble-fingered rogue soon managed to relieve him of the key necessary to open the iron-grated door of his cell. Tom slid quietly into the narrow passage and down the stairs to the yard. He had the cheek to enter the turnkey's apartment and steal a silver tankard worth £10 before making his getaway over the prison wall.

Since he needed a horse, he stole one, complete with saddle and bridle, from the first stable he came across, before riding hell-for-leather towards Bath. Soon he was kicking the dust of Somerset off his heels as he crossed the border into Gloucestershire.

Tom was eventually caught after robbing a farmer on Hounslow Heath; he was thrown into Newgate prison to await trial at the Old Bailey. This time, luck deserted him; he was found guilty and sentenced to death. On 3rd June 1691, he was carried from Newgate in an open cart, his coffin next to him, accompanied by the hangman and a chaplain. The handsome highwayman, still immaculately dressed in his favourite white waistcoat and breeches and sporting a hat adorned with cherry-coloured ribbons, was cheered wildly by the excitable mob and showered with flowers by sobbing ladies watching the grim procession from upstairs windows.

He made one last frantic protest before the noose was placed round his neck - he tried to kick both the chaplain and the executioner out of the cart! Jonathan Swift described the event in *Going to be Hanged* (1727):

'And when his last speech the loud hawkers did cry
He swore from his cart "It was all a damn'd lie!"
The hangman for pardon fell down on his knee;
Tom gave him a kick in the guts for his fee.'

Minutes later, Tom Cox was launched into Eternity. He was just twenty-five years old.